simply-built furniture

Danny Proulx

POPULAR WOODWORKING BOOKS
CINCINNATI, OHIO
www.popularwoodworking.com

READ THIS IMPORTANT SAFETY NOTICE

To prevent accidents, keep safety in mind while you work. Use the safety guards installed on power equipment; they are for your protection.

When working on power equipment, keep fingers away from saw blades, wear safety goggles to prevent injuries from flying wood chips and sawdust, wear hearing protection and consider installing a dust vacuum to reduce the amount of airborne sawdust in your woodshop.

Don't wear loose clothing, such as neckties or shirts with loose sleeves, or jewelry, such as rings, necklaces or bracelets, when working on power equipment. Tie back long hair to prevent it from getting caught in your equipment.

People who are sensitive to certain chemicals should check the chemical content of any product before using it.

Due to the variability of local conditions, construction materials, skill levels, etc., neither the author nor Popular Woodworking Books assumes any responsibility for any accidents, injuries, damages or other losses incurred resulting from the material presented in this book.

The authors and editors who compiled this book have tried to make the contents as accurate and correct as possible. Plans, illustrations, photographs and text have been carefully checked. All instructions, plans and projects should be carefully read, studied and understood before beginning construction.

Prices listed for supplies and equipment were current at the time of publication and are subject to change.

METRIC CONVERSION CHART

TO CONVERT	TO	MULTIPLY BY
Inches	Centimeters	2.54
Centimeters	Inches	0.4
Feet	Centimeters	30.5
Centimeters	Feet	0.03
Yards	Meters	0.9
Meters	Yards	1.1

Distributed in Canada by Fraser Direct
100 Armstrong Avenue
Georgetown, Ontario L7G 5S4
Canada

Distributed in the U.K. and Europe by F+W Media International
Brunel House
Newton Abbot
Devon TQ12 4PU
England
Tel: (+44) 1626 323200
Fax: (+44) 1626 323319
E-mail: postmaster@davidandcharles.co.uk

Distributed in Australia by Capricorn Link
P.O. Box 704
Windsor, NSW 2756
Australia

Visit our Web site at www.popularwoodworking.com.

Other fine Popular Woodworking Books are available from your local bookstore or direct from the publisher.

14   13   12   11   5   4   3   2

Library of Congress Cataloging-in-Publication Data

Proulx, Danny, 1947-
  Simply-built furniture : 25 practical projects for your home / by Danny Proulx. -- 1st ed.
    p. cm.
  ISBN 978-1-4403-1036-2 (pbk. : alk. paper)
  1. Furniture making--Amateurs' manuals. 2. Woodwork--Amateurs' manuals. I. Title.
  TT195.P768 2010
  684'.08--dc22
                    2010028078

ACQUISITIONS EDITOR: David Thiel
SENIOR EDITOR: Jim Stack
DESIGNER: Brian Roeth
PRODUCTION COORDINATOR: Mark Griffin
PHOTOGRAPHERS: Danny Proulx, Michael Bowie,
    LUX Photographic Services, Inc.
ILLUSTRATOR: Len Churchill

ABOUT THE AUTHOR

For over 15 years, Danny shared with us his passion for woodworking through his books, magazine articles and website advice, as well as through teaching and mentoring his students and clients. He founded Rideau Cabinet in 1989 and started building kitchens and specialty cabinets. Over time, Danny married his love of woodworking and writing with his photographic skills and wrote 15 books during a period of 9 years. He also wrote for several magazines including *Canadian Woodworking* and *CabinetMaker Magazine*. He started giving seminars in his home for new woodworkers and eventually started teaching courses at Algonquin College in Ottawa, Ontario.

table of contents

introduction

Danny Proulx was a multi-faceted individual who knew how to build cabinets, furniture and could write clearly and concisely, while at the same time sounding like he was right there in your shop giving you instructions.

We've chosen 26 projects from some of Danny's books. These projects are straight-forward designs that will fit almost any decor.

Keeping it simple is what this book is all about. The projects in *Simply-Built Furniture* can be made using basic power woodworking tools: a pocket-hole drilling jig, a biscuit joiner, a table saw and a drill press. Plus, some hand tools: a chisel, battery screwdriver, hammer, etc.

Several of the projects are built in sections that are then assembled to create the final piece. This can serve several purposes. It's easier to transport several small parts than one big one and, if you have a small woodworking shop like most of us do, you will appreciate having to built only one or two pieces of a project at one time. When these are finished, then can be moved to create more room in your shop so you can continue building.

The materials for these furniture projects can be found at most home centers. Danny designed his projects so the materials can simply be cut to size and assembled. You don't need a planer or jointer to prepare the hardwood parts. The sheets goods can be cut to size using several different tools. A table saw is best, but a straight-edge used with a circular saw will get the job done too. And, if all you have is a jig saw, well, that will work also.

Danny preferred tools with cords and batteries, because they are efficient and he could get more work done in a shorter amount of time. If you are able to only work weekends on your woodworking projects, power tools are your best friends — your work will progress quickly and efficiently.

Simply-Built Furniture has a project for every room in your house, so choose which project you'd like to build and keep it simple.

sofa & hall tables

The design for this table came from fellow woodworker Michael Brazeau of Milton, Ontario. He built a beautiful Shaker hall table with inset-style drawers and lovely tapered legs. I asked Michael if I could use his design for my book, and he agreed.

I've changed a few things in Michael's design, but retained his original concept. I decided to use overlay drawer faces and altered his drawer box guide system slightly. My table legs are also tapered, which adds greatly to the beauty of this design.

This project is called a sofa or hall table because it's equally useful behind a sofa in an area where the sofa isn't placed against a wall. If you have room in your entrance hall or foyer, this table will certainly impress your visitors. Hang a mirror over the table in your entrance way and you'll have a useful spot to rest your shopping bags or leave messages for family members.

The leg tapers appear complicated, but they are surprisingly simple to cut. There are many low-cost tapering jigs on the market, and the process is nothing more than a variation of straight cutting on the table saw. The top is detailed with a cove cut on the bottom, which lightens the overall appearance of the table. And like all the projects in this book, pocket hole joinery is the primary construction method used.

This appears to be a complicated design with coved top and tapered legs, when, in reality, it's simple to build. This project will draw a lot of comments because the two tapered profiles on each leg create a powerful visual statement.

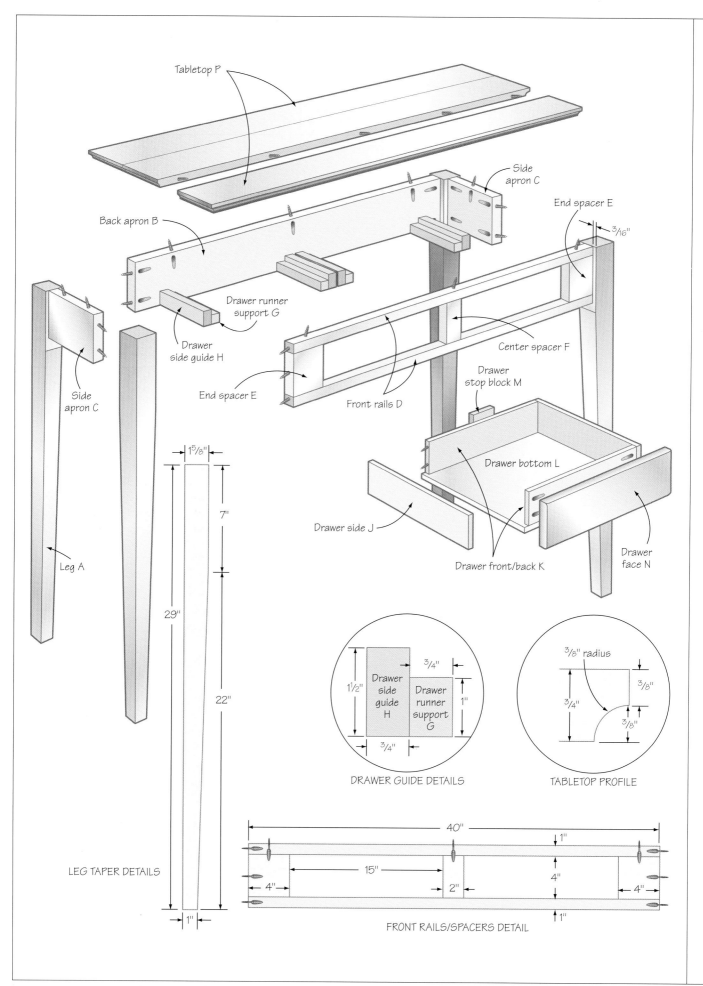

Tabletop P

Side apron C

End spacer E

3/16"

Back apron B

Drawer runner support G

Center spacer F

Side apron C

Drawer side guide H

Drawer stop block M

End spacer E

Front rails D

Drawer bottom L

Drawer side J

Leg A

Drawer front/back K

Drawer face N

1⁵/₈"

7"

29"

22"

1"

LEG TAPER DETAILS

1¹/₂"   3/4"

Drawer side guide H   Drawer runner support G

1"

3/4"

DRAWER GUIDE DETAILS

3/8" radius

3/4"   3/8"

3/8"

TABLETOP PROFILE

40"   1"

15"   4"

4"   2"   4"

1"

FRONT RAILS/SPACERS DETAIL

REFERENCE	QUANTITY	PART	STOCK	THICKNESS	(mm)	WIDTH	(mm)	LENGTH	(mm)	COMMENTS
A	4	legs	hardwood	$1^5/_8$	(41)	$1^5/_8$	(41)	29	(737)	taper
B	1	back apron	hardwood	$^3/_4$	(19)	6	(152)	40	(1016)	
C	2	side aprons	hardwood	$^3/_4$	(19)	6	(152)	7	(178)	
D	2	front rails	hardwood	$^3/_4$	(19)	1	(25)	40	(1016)	
E	2	end spacers	hardwood	$^3/_4$	(19)	4	(102)	4	(102)	
F	1	center spacer	hardwood	$^3/_4$	(19)	2	(51)	4	(102)	
G	4	drawer runner supports	hardwood	$^3/_4$	(19)	1	(25)	$7^7/_8$	(200)	
H	4	drawer side guides	hardwood	$^3/_4$	(19)	$1^1/_2$	(38)	$7^7/_8$	(200)	
J	4	drawer sides	Baltic birch	$^1/_2$	(13)	3	(76)	8	(203)	
K	4	drawer backs and fronts	Baltic birch	$^1/_2$	(13)	3	(76)	$13^7/_8$	(352)	
L	2	drawer bottoms	Baltic birch	$^1/_2$	(13)	8	(203)	$14^7/_8$	(378)	
M	2	drawer stops	Baltic birch	$^1/_2$	(13)	3	(76)	2	(51)	
N	2	drawer faces	hardwood	$^3/_4$	(19)	5	(127)	16	(406)	
P	1	tabletop	hardwood	$^3/_4$	(19)	$12^1/_2$	(318)	$47^1/_4$	(1200)	

HARDWARE AND SUPPLIES

Pocket hole screws: $1^1/_4$ (32mm), 1" (25mm)

Wood screws: $1^1/_2$ (38mm), 1" (25mm)

Brad nails

Glue

Drawer knobs

1 The four legs A are made using standard $1^5/_8$"-square stock, cut 29" long. The taper on two adjoining sides of each leg begins 7" from the top and tapers from $1^5/_8$" to 1" at the bottom. Mark the tapered cut sides to make assembly easier and error-proof. Tapering jigs are easy to make, and there are a number of plans in books about shop jig construction. However, a taper jig is an inexpensive tool costing about $20. Follow the details in the drawing, and make a few test-cuts with scrap lumber before beginning the final cut on each leg. Remember this important note: Two adjoining faces on each leg should be tapered. That will allow us to attach the skirt boards to the legs with tapers facing inward or toward each other.

2 The two sides C and back B aprons are solid hardwood. Cut them to the sizes indicated in the materials list, then drill two pocket holes in each end on all three boards. Before beginning the assembly steps, drill three pocket holes on the upper inside edge of the back apron and two in the side aprons. These holes will be used to secure the tabletop. Join the three aprons to the legs with glue and $1^1/_4$"-long pocket hole screws. Inset the aprons on each leg by $^3/_16$". Remember, the two side tapers on each leg face inward and toward each other. Use the offset jig that was described in chapter two when attaching the aprons.

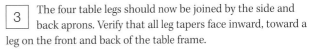

3 The four table legs should now be joined by the side and back aprons. Verify that all leg tapers face inward, toward a leg on the front and back of the table frame.

4 | Prepare the front rails D and spacers E and F, as detailed in the materials list. Glue the rails to the spacers, following the drawing detail, and secure with 1½"-long wood screws to form the front apron assembly. Note: Cut all the front apron assembly pieces from one board and maintain their position as parts of the whole board. By keeping them in order, the cut boards, once assembled, will appear as one board because the grain pattern was maintained.

5 | The front apron should have two pocket holes drilled on each end. As well, drill three holes along the top edge that will be used to secure the tabletop. Once the front apron drilling is finished, it can be attached to the legs with glue and 1¼" pocket hole screws. The front apron assembly should also be inset ³⁄₁₆" back from the front face of each leg.

6 | Build the four drawer runner assemblies, using the runner supports G and side guides H. The assemblies are constructed using glue and brad nails. Runner assemblies are set flush with the top edge of the lower rail and front apron spacers. Drill pocket holes in the bottom edge of side guides H, and attach the assemblies with 1¼" pocket hole screws and glue.

7 | The four drawer runner assemblies should be aligned as shown.

8 | I am using ½"-thick Baltic birch, sometimes called cabinet-grade plywood, to build two drawer boxes. The overall size of these drawer boxes will be ⅛" narrower than the drawer openings in the front rail, and 3½" high. Cut all the drawer box parts J, K and L to the sizes indicated in the materials list. Then, drill two pocket holes on each end of the outside faces on the fronts and backs K. Remember to set your pocket hole drill-stop guide for ½"-thick material. Attach the fronts and backs to the sides with 1" pocket hole screws and glue. The bottoms L are secured with glue and brad nails.

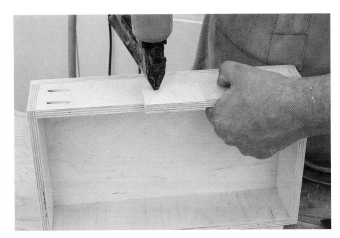

9   Install the two drawer stops M on the backboard of each drawer box. These stops are attached with glue and brad nails, and are 1" above the top edge of the backboards. They are used to prevent the drawer from being pulled all the way out.

10   The two drawer faces N are solid wood with their front face edges rounded over using a ¼" roundover router bit. They are aligned on the box so they extend ½" beyond the drawer opening on all edges of the front apron. Use 1"-long wood screws, driven from the inside of the drawer box, to attach the faces.

11   Glue up enough boards to form the finished tabletop P, measuring 12½" deep by 47¼" long. Use 1¼" pocket hole screws and glue to join the boards.

12   Use a cove bit to profile the lower edge of the tabletop. Cut the cove just deep enough to leave a ⅜"-high straight edge on the top side. Before attaching the top, enlarge the screw shaft-hole diameter of the pocket holes to provide expansion room for the solid-wood top. The screw hole should be double the screw shaft diameter.

13   Attach the top using 1¼" pocket hole screws in the previously drilled pocket holes. There should be an overhang of 2" on each end and 1⅛" on the front and back side of the table. All overhang dimensions are measured from the leg faces to the tabletop edges. Notice that the cove cut is on the underside of the tabletop after installation.

rustic pine chest of drawers

This rustic pine chest is easy to build. With five large drawers, it can hold a great deal of clothing. The chest is a low-cost solution to organizing a child's bedroom. But don't stop with the chest; it's only the beginning. A matching dresser and armoire can be easily built in the same style by altering a few dimensions.

Traditional, country or rustic pine furniture is simplicity at its best. The drawers are solid wood with an applied drawer front. They slide on wood frames that — with a little paste wax applied once a year — work very well. No fancy hardware here, just solid wood.

The top and sides are glued-up ¾"- thick pine boards. The techniques for creating these panels are described in chapter 1, page 16. I'm using #1 and #2 pine, which is relatively inexpensive.

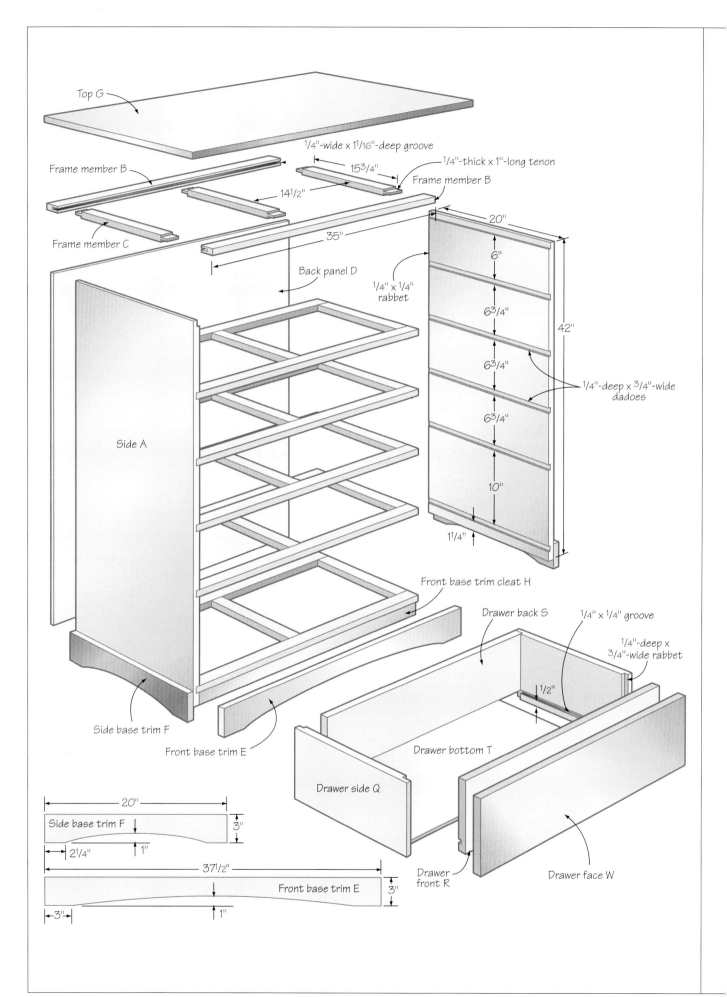

Top G

$1/4"$-wide x $1^{1}/16"$-deep groove

Frame member B

$15^{3}/4"$

$1/4"$-thick x $1"$-long tenon

Frame member B

$14^{1}/2"$

Frame member C

$35"$

Back panel D

$1/4" \times 1/4"$ rabbet

$20"$

$6"$

$6^{3}/4"$

$6^{3}/4"$

$42"$

$6^{3}/4"$

$1/4"$-deep x $3/4"$-wide dadoes

$10"$

Side A

$1^{1}/4"$

Front base trim cleat H

Drawer back S

$1/4" \times 1/4"$ groove

$1/4"$-deep x $3/4"$-wide rabbet

$1/2"$

Drawer bottom T

Side base trim F

Front base trim E

Drawer side Q

$20"$

Side base trim F

$3"$

$2^{1}/4"$

$1"$

$37^{1}/2"$

Front base trim E

$3"$

$3"$

$1"$

Drawer front R

Drawer face W

RUSTIC PINE CHEST OF DRAWERS | INCHES (MILLIMETERS)

REFERENCE	QUANTITY	PART	STOCK	THICKNESS	(mm)	WIDTH	(mm)	LENGTH	(mm)
A	2	sides	solid wood	$3/4$	(19)	20	(508)	42	(1067)
B	12	frame members	solid wood	$3/4$	(19)	2	(51)	35	(889)
C	18	frame members	solid wood	$3/4$	(19)	2	(51)	$17^3/_4$	(451)
D	1	back panel	plywood	$1/4$	(6)	35	(889)	41	(1041)
E	1	front base trim	solid wood	$3/4$	(19)	3	(76)	$37^1/_2$	(953)
F	2	side base trim	solid wood	$3/4$	(19)	3	(76)	20	(508)
G	1	top	solid wood	$3/4$	(19)	21	(533)	38	(965)
H	1	front base trim cleat	solid wood	$3/4$	(19)	$1^1/_4$	(32)	$34^1/_2$	(876)
J	2	drawer sides	solid wood	$3/4$	(19)	$5^7/_8$	(149)	$19^1/_2$	(495)
K	1	drawer front	solid wood	$3/4$	(19)	$5^7/_8$	(149)	$33^3/_8$	(848)
L	1	drawer back	solid wood	$3/4$	(19)	$5^1/_8$	(130)	$33^3/_8$	(848)
M	6	drawer sides	solid wood	$3/4$	(19)	$6^5/_8$	(168)	$19^1/_2$	(495)
N	3	drawer fronts	solid wood	$3/4$	(19)	$6^5/_8$	(168)	$33^3/_8$	(848)
P	3	drawer backs	solid wood	$3/4$	(19)	$5^7/_8$	(149)	$33^3/_8$	(848)
Q	2	drawer sides	solid wood	$3/4$	(19)	$9^7/_8$	(251)	$19^1/_2$	(495)
R	1	drawer front	solid wood	$3/4$	(19)	$9^7/_8$	(251)	$33^3/_8$	(848)
S	1	drawer back	solid wood	$3/4$	(19)	$9^1/_8$	(232)	$33^3/_8$	(848)
T	5	drawer bottoms	plywood	$1/4$	(6)	19	(483)	$33^3/_8$	(848)
U	1	drawer face	solid wood	$3/4$	(19)	$6^1/_2$	(165)	35	(889)
V	3	drawer faces	solid wood	$3/4$	(19)	$7^1/_4$	(184)	35	(889)
W	1	drawer face	solid wood	$3/4$	(19)	$10^1/_2$	(267)	35	(889)

HARDWARE AND SUPPLIES

glue

brad nails

2" (51mm) screws

1¼" (32mm) screws

wood plugs

finishing nails

drawer pulls

1   Glue up and cut the two sides A to a finished size of ¾" thick by 20" wide by 42" high. Use a stacked carbide-tipped dado cutter to form the dadoes as well as the back rabbets on the inside face of each side panel. The dadoes are all ¾" wide and ¼" deep. The rabbet to receive the plywood back panel D is also ¼" deep, but it has to be only ¼" wide. If you don't have a dado blade on your table saw, use a router and straight ¾" cutting bit. The rabbet can also be completed with this straight bit, but you should have a guide system to limit the width to ¼".

2   Cut all the frame members B and C to the sizes indicated in the materials list. The shorter members require a ¼"-thick by 1"-long by 2"-wide tenon on each end. The long members require a ¼"-wide by 1"-deep groove on one long edge. The grooves, as well as the tenons, can be cut with a dado blade on your table saw. However, both types of cuts can also be made with a standard blade in the saw; it's a little slower but can be done with multiple passes.

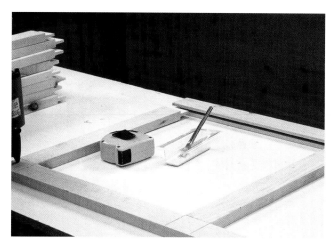

3   Build the frames as shown in the illustration. The six frames are the same size and constructed in the same manner. Apply glue to each tenon and slide the tenon into the groove. One short frame member is at either end of the long frame member, and the third rail is in the center. Secure the joints with two small brad nails to provide support while the glue sets.

4   Attach the frame assemblies to the sides A. Use glue and small brad nails to secure the frames in the dado cuts. Frame members can be pinned in place by toe nailing. Be careful not to drive the nail through the face of the side panel.

5   The back panel D is glued and nailed into the rabbet on each side A. Nail one side, then check that the cabinet is square by measuring the diagonals. Adjust if necessary, and complete the nailing.

6   The base trim consists of boards E and F, cut to the dimensions shown. Cut the lower arcs in each trim board as shown in the illustration, using a band saw or jigsaw. Sand the trim boards smooth. Before installing the front base trim E, glue the front base trim cleat H under, and at the front edge, of the lower frame. Secure the base trim to the chest, using glue and 1¼" screws from inside the chest case. Note that the 2¼" straight edge on the side base trim butts against the front base trim. The ¾" thickness of the front base trim when added to the side base trim, creates a 3"-wide foot on the front and side faces. The boards are installed 1½" up from the bottom edge of the chest sides. Now, round over the top edge of the trim boards with a ¼" roundover bit in a router. If you don't have a router, ease the edges with sandpaper.

8 | Build the drawer box so it's ⅛" narrower than the opening and ⅛" less in height. The drawer faces are ½" wider and taller than the openings. Cut all the drawer parts. The drawer front and sides require a ¼"-wide by ¼" deep groove that begins ½" up from the bottom edges. The drawer sides also require a ¼"-deep rabbet that's ¾" wide on both ends. The rabbets are on the inside face of each drawer side and will receive the drawer front and back. Attach the sides to the back and front, in the rabbets, with glue and finishing nails. The top edges of all boards are flush with each other. The back's bottom edge should end at the top of the grooves so bottom can be inserted.

7 | Construct a glued-up panel to make the top G. Round over the top and bottom edges of the front and sides with a ⅜" roundover bit. Secure the top with 1¼" screws through the top frame.

9 | From the back of the drawer, slide the ¼"-thick plywood bottom into the grooves. It should fit snug in the side grooves and go all the way into the front groove. The back's bottom edge will be completely covered when the plywood bottom is seated in the front groove. Nail the bottom board to the back's edge. Do not use glue.

10 | Install the drawer box in the cabinet. Round over the front edges of the drawer face and secure it in place. It should overlap the opening by ¼" on all edges. Attach the face with four 1¼" screws through the inside of the drawer box.

7-drawer chest

Bedrooms never have enough drawer space. Most of us have undergarments, socks, T-shirts and other clothing items that are ideally suited for drawer storage. So, improve the situation in your children's bedroom, or even your own, and build this project.

This high chest has seven relatively shallow drawers. You can make the same project with deeper drawers, but there will not be as many drawers. But no matter what the size, all chests are built in basically the same fashion. Once you're built one like the one in this chapter, you will be able to build a size to suit your specific needs.

Many woodworkers feel a great deal of skill is needed to build a chest or dresser. Nothing could be farther from the truth. It is a simple process. Take your time and perform each step in order. You'll soon see how easy it is to build great-looking bedroom furniture.

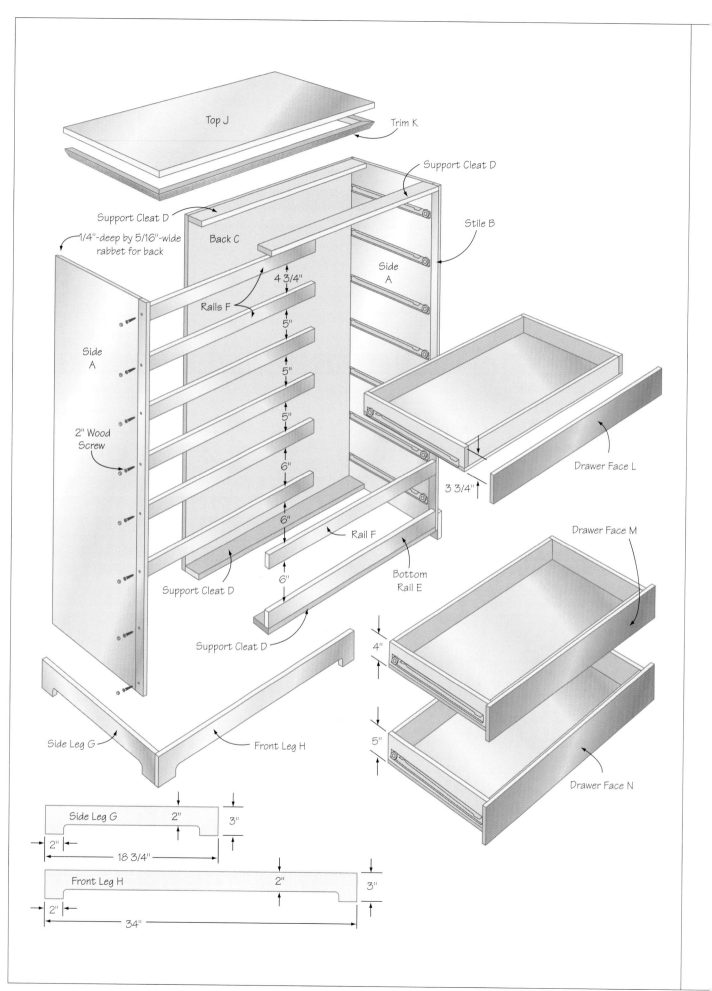

Top J

Trim K

Support Cleat D

Support Cleat D

Stile B

1/4"-deep by 5/16"-wide rabbet for back

Back C

Side A

Side A

4 3/4"

Rails F

5"

5"

5"

2" Wood Screw

6"

6"

Drawer Face L

3 3/4"

Rail F

Bottom Rail E

6"

Support Cleat D

Support Cleat D

Drawer Face M

4"

Side Leg G

Front Leg H

5"

Drawer Face N

Side Leg G   2"   3"

2"

18 3/4"

Front Leg H   2"   3"

2"

34"

REFERENCE	QUANTITY	PART	STOCK	THICKNESS	(mm)	WIDTH	(mm)	LENGTH	(mm)
A	2	sides	veneer PB	$^{11}/_{16}$	(18)	18	(457)	52	(1320)
B	2	stiles	hardwood	$^{11}/_{16}$	(18)	$^3/_4$	(19)	52	(1320)
C	1	back	veneer PB	$^1/_4$	(6)	$31^3/_4$	(806)	52	(1320)
D	4	support cleats	veneer PB	$^{11}/_{16}$	(18)	$2^1/_2$	(64)	$31^1/_8$	(791)
E	1	bottom rail	hardwood	$^3/_4$	(19)	$2^1/_4$	(57)	$31^1/_8$	(791)
F	7	rails	hardwood	$^3/_4$	(19)	$1^1/_2$	(76)	$31^1/_8$	(791)
G	2	side legs	hardwood	$^3/_4$	(19)	3	(76)	$18^3/_4$	(476)
H	1	front leg	hardwood	$^3/_4$	(19)	3	(24)	34	(864)
J	1	top	hardwood	$^3/_4$	(19)	$19^1/_2$	(1524)	$34^1/_2$	(876)
K	1	moulding	hardwood	$^3/_4$	(19)	1	(25)	96	(2438)
L	1	drawer face	hardwood	$^3/_4$	(19)	$5^1/_4$	(133)	32	(813)
M	3	drawer faces	hardwood	$^3/_4$	(19)	$5^1/_2$	(140)	32	(813)
N	3	drawer faces	hardwood	$^3/_4$	(19)	$6^1/_2$	(165)	32	(813)
TALL DRAWER BOXES									
	6	sides	hardwood	$^1/_2$	(13)	$3^1/_2$	(89)	18	(457)
	6	backs & fronts	hardwood	$^1/_2$	(13)	$3^1/_2$	(89)	$29^1/_8$	(740)
	3	bottoms	hardwood	$^1/_2$	(13)	18	(457)	$30^1/_8$	(765)
TALL DRAWER BOXES									
	6	sides	hardwood	$^1/_2$	(13)	$4^1/_2$	(114)	18	(457)
	6	backs & fronts	hardwood	$^1/_2$	(13)	$4^1/_2$	(114)	$29^1/_8$	(740)
	3	bottoms	hardwood	$^1/_2$	(13)	18	(457)	$30^1/_8$	(765)
TALL DRAWER BOXES									
	2	sides	hardwood	$^1/_2$	(13)	$3^1/_4$	(83)	18	(457)
	2	backs & fronts	hardwood	$^1/_2$	(13)	$3^1/_4$	(83)	$29^1/_8$	(740)
	1	bottoms	hardwood	$^1/_2$	(13)	18	(457)	$30^1/_8$	(765)

HARDWARE AND SUPPLIES

7- drawer pulls

7 sets - 18" bottom-mounted drawer slides

1", $1^1/_4$", and 2" wood screws

2"finish nails

brad nails

$^3/_4$" wood plugs

carpenter's wood glue

wood filler

1   Cut the two side panels A to size. Then cut a $^1/_4$"-deep by $^1/_4$"-wide rabbet on the back inside face of both side panels to receive the back. (The rabbet can be cut with a hand held router, a router table or a table saw equipped with a dado blade.)

2   Use glue and 2" finishing nails to secure the stiles B. Countersink the nail heads and fill the holes with colored filler that will match the final finish.

4 Attach the bottom rail E with glue and screws through the side panels and bottom cleat. Use 2" screws in predrilled holes for the maximum holding power.

3 Cut and attache the four support cleats D. Then fir the back into the rabbets and attach it with glue and brad nails through the rear and into each side panel. Since I want my chest carcass to have a finished width of 32½", my back is 31¾" plus the remaining thickness of each side panel after the rabbets have been cut.

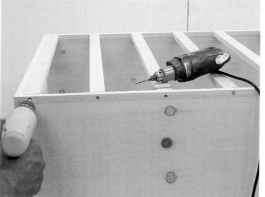

5 Attach the remaining seven rails F with glue and screws through the outside of each stile. Use 2" screws in predrilled counterbored holes so wood plugs can be installed. (One screw per side is adequate.) Make sure the placement of the rails allow for three bottom drawers that are 6" high, three middle drawers that are 5" high and a top drawer that is 4¾" high.

8 Make a solid wood top panel J using three ¾"-thick boards edge-glued together. If you haven't got the equipment to edge-glue, premade solid wood panels that can be cut to size are available at most large home centers.

6 Cut out each leg G, round over the top, bottom and back edges with a ¼" router bit, and install each leg 1½" up from the bottom edge of the side panels. Use glue and four 1¼" screws through the inside of the cabinet side panels.

7 Cut out the front leg H, round over all edges of the outside face and attach it with glue and 1¼" screws.

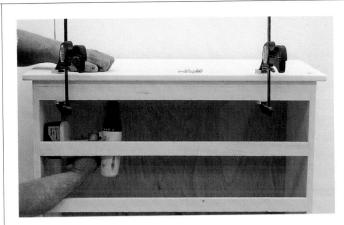

9 Cut the top to a finished size, and round over the top and bottom face of the sides and front with a ¼" roundover bit in a router. Secure the top to the cabinet, making sure it's flush with the back. Use glue and 1¼" screws through the cleats to anchor the top. If you're using a solid wood top, don't use glue. The boards will expand and contract with humidity changes, and the screw-only method will allow a slight bit of room for movement.

10 Install ¾"-thick by 1"-high trim moulding K under the chest top. Dozens of styles are available, so choose one that matches the cabinet style.

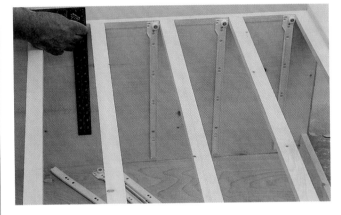

11 Build the drawer from ½" Baltic birch plywood. Use the sizes detailed in the materials list, and follow the steps outlined in chapter two. To install the bottom-mount drawer glides, first determine the height of the screw line above each rail for your particular brand of drawer glides. (The Blum drawer glides I use are installed by drawing a center screw line on the side panel ¾" above the rail.) Lay the chest carcass on its back and use a carpenter's square to draw a straight line to indicate the center of each screw hole. Install one ¾" screw in the front and one at the back (in the adjusting screw hole) of each glide. Inset the remaining screws once you test the drawers. If slight adjustment is necessary, loosen the back screw and align the glide.

12 Check the fit and alignment of each drawer box. If a box doesn't sit properly on the glides, adjust it by slightly raising or lowering one side rail. Once the drawers are correct, install the remaining rail screws.

13 Round over the outside edges of the drawer faces L, M and N with a ¼" roundover bit. Secure each face to the drawer box using four 1" screws. Since the top drawer face can't be attached by reaching through the next higher drawer box space, drill the hole for the hardware you plan on using, and temporarily attach the drawer face to the box using a 1¼" screw through the hardware hole. The drawer can then be opened with the face securely in place. Once the face is attached from the inside, remove the screw from the front and install the hardware.

bed with storage

This platform storage bed project is a great addition to any child's or teenager's room. It features a bookcase headboard and four large storage drawers.

The bed is built of knotty pine in the rustic or country style. The dimensions given are to accommodate a standard twin mattress measuring 39" wide by 75" long.

I've also detailed a construction method using knockdown hardware. The cap bolts used here can be removed and replaced when the bed is moved.

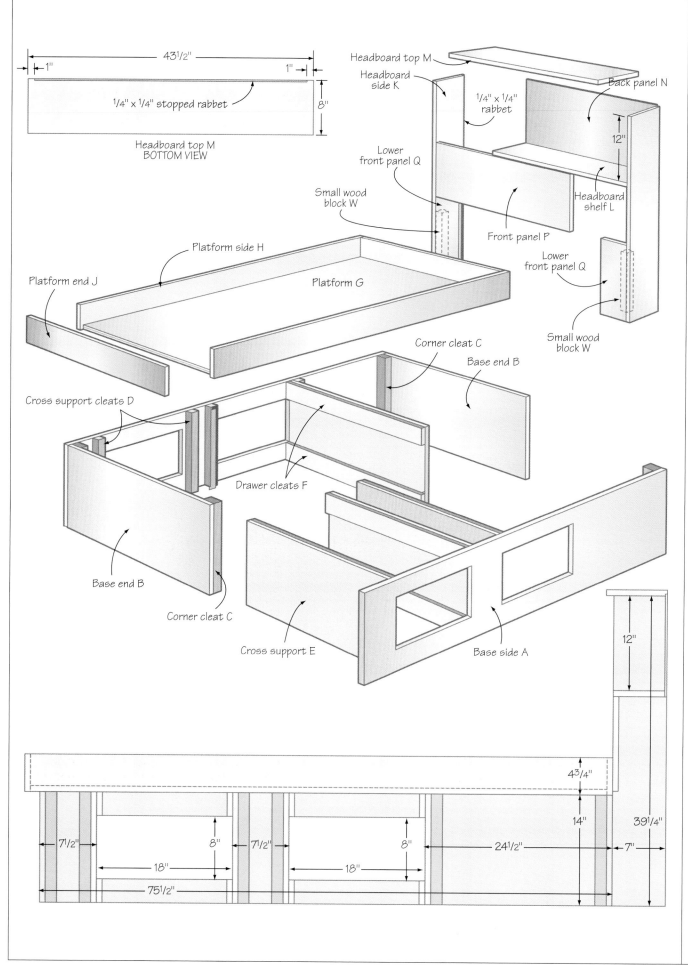

43½"

1"

1"

¼" × ¼" stopped rabbet

8"

Headboard top M
BOTTOM VIEW

Headboard top M

Headboard
side K

¼" × ¼"
rabbet

Back panel N

12"

Lower
front panel Q

Small wood
block W

Headboard
shelf L

Front panel P

Platform side H

Lower
front panel Q

Platform end J

Platform G

Small wood
block W

Corner cleat C

Base end B

Cross support cleats D

Drawer cleats F

Base end B

Corner cleat C

Cross support E

Base side A

12"

4¾"

7½"

8"

7½"

8"

24½"

14"

39¼"

18"

18"

7"

75½"

30

REFERENCE	QUANTITY	PART	STOCK	THICKNESS	(mm)	WIDTH	(mm)	LENGTH	(mm)
A	2	base sides	solid wood	3/4	(19)	14	(356)	75½	(1918)
B	2	base ends	solid wood	3/4	(19)	14	(356)	36	(914)
C	4	corner cleats	solid wood	1½	(38)	2¼	(57)	14	(356)
D	8	cross support cleats	solid wood	1½	(38)	1½	(38)	14	(356)
E	4	cross supports	plywood	3/4	(19)	14	(356)	36	(914)
F	8	drawer cleats	solid wood	3/4	(19)	3	(76)	36	(914)
G	1	platform	plywood	3/4	(19)	40	(1016)	76	(1930)
H	2	platform sides	solid wood	3/4	(19)	4¾	(121)	77½	(1969)
J	2	platform ends	solid wood	3/4	(19)	4¾	(121)	40	(1016)
K	2	headboard sides	solid wood	3/4	(19)	7	(178)	39¼	(997)
L	1	headboard shelf	solid wood	3/4	(19)	6¾	(171)	40	(1016)
M	1	headboard top	solid wood	3/4	(19)	8	(203)	43½	(1105)
N	1	back panel	plywood	¼	(6)	13	(330)	40½	(1029)
P	1	front panel	solid wood	3/4	(19)	12	(305)	40	(1016)
Q	2	lower front panels	solid wood	3/4	(19)	7¼	(184)	14½	(368)
R	8	drawer sides	solid wood	3/4	(19)	7⅞	(200)	17	(432)
S	4	drawer fronts	solid wood	3/4	(19)	7⅞	(200)	16⅞	(429)
T	4	drawer backs	solid wood	3/4	(19)	7⅛	(181)	16⅞	(429)
U	4	drawer bottoms	plywood	¼	(6)	16½	(419)	16⅞	(429)
V	4	drawer faces	solid wood	3/4	(19)	8½	(216)	18½	(470)
W	2	small wood blocks	solid wood	3/4	(19)	3/4	(19)	12	(305)

HARDWARE AND SUPPLIES

glue

2" (51mm) wood screws

cap bolts

1¼" (32mm) screws

wood plugs

brad nails

drawer pulls

---

1 The base sides A and base ends B are two-board glue-ups using pine. I made my panels using stock 1×8 wood and edge-gluing as detailed under "Making Solid Wood Panel Glue-Ups" in chapter 1, page 16. Once the base sides

A were glued into a panel and cut to size, I cut out the two drawer openings in each one as shown in the illustration. I could have built the base sides with individual boards, but since it would mean assembling a lot of small pieces to form each base side, this cutout method seemed to be the most practical solution. The base ends B for the bed frame are also two-board glue-ups. Follow the directions on edge gluing wood, then cut each panel to size and cut out the drawer openings on the base sides with a jigsaw and fine-tooth blade. You can minimize edge chipping with your jigsaw by first using a sharp knife to score the cut lines. Attach the 8 cross-support cleats D on the inside face of the base sides A. Each cleat is secured with glue and 2" screws, ¾" back from each drawer opening. Each side of the four openings should have one cleat.

2 Using glue and 2" wood screws, attach the corner cleats C to the inside face of each base end B. The 2¼" face of the cleat is installed flush with the outside edge of each base end B. Use knockdown fasteners, called cap bolts, to join the sides A and ends B at each corner. These are easily removed and replaced if the bed has to been taken apart.

3 Four cross supports E will be used to strengthen the base and provide runners for the drawers. The cross supports are ¾"-thick plywood or particleboard, 14" high by 36" wide. Each cross support requires a 3"-high drawer cleat F on the top and bottom to form tracks and top runners for the drawers. Use glue and 1¼" screws to attach the drawer cleats F to the cross supports E.

4 Screw the cross support assemblies to the cross support cleats D with 2" screws. Do not glue these in place, so they can be removed when dismantling the bed. Notice that the drawer cleats face into each drawer space.

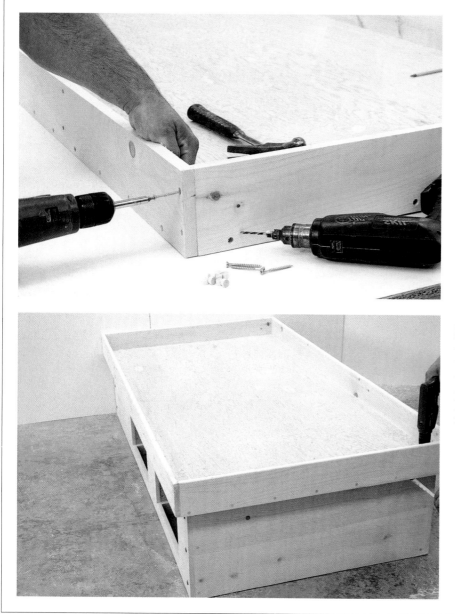

5 Cut the plywood platform G, platform sides H and platform ends J as detailed in the materials list. Join the ends J to the platform G, and then attach the sides H. Use glue with 2" wood screws in counterbored holes that are filled with wood plugs. The bottom face of platform G is attached flush with the bottom edges of the sides H and ends J. The overall outside dimension of the frame should be 41½" wide by 77½" long.

6 Secure the mattress platform to the base with 2" screws through the plywood into the corner cleats C. The headboard end of the frame is flush with the base. The sides and footboard end overhang the base by 2". Do not use glue, so the platform can be removed if the bed has to be moved.

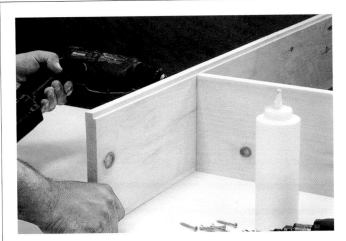

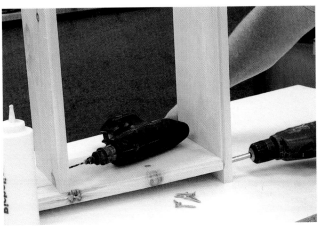

7 | Cut all the headboard pieces, K, L, M, N, P and Q, as detailed in the materials list. Before beginning the assembly, cut a ¼"-deep by ¼"-wide rabbet on the back inside face of the two headboard sides K. Join the sides to the shelf L, 12" down from the top edges of sides K, with glue and 2" wood screws. Install the screws from the outside and fill the counterbored holes with wood plugs.

8 | Round over the front and end edges of the top M. Use a ¼" roundover bit on the top and bottom of each edge. The top also requires a stopped rabbet that's ¼" wide by ¼" deep to receive the back panel N. A stopped rabbet is a cut that stops 1" short of the board's ends. This will prevent the rabbet from being seen on the underside of the top at either end. Secure the top M to the sides K with glue and 2" wood screws in plugged holes. Ensure the sides K are spaced 40" apart and the top M extends 1" past each side. The top should overhang the front edge and be aligned flush with the back edges of the sides.

9 | Install the ¼" back panel N with glue and brad nails in the rabbet cuts. The front panel P rests tight to the underside of shelf L. It is secured with glue and 2" wood screws in plugged holes through the sides and shelf. The front panel should be installed flush with the front edges of the sides and shelf.

10 | The two lower front panels Q are needed to hide the space between the headboard sides and the base. Join them flush with the front edge of side K and tight to the bottom edge of front panel P. Use 1¼" wood screws and glue. I've also used a small wood block W to support the lower top front panel joint. Install this block behind the joint, using glue and screws. Attach the headboard assembly to the base with screws through the back of the lower front panels Q and into the base end B. Build the drawers with panels R, S, T, U and V, following the steps outlined in "Building Rustic Pine Drawers" in this chapter. These drawers will slide on the drawer cleats F.

wardrobe storage cabinet

The wardrobe project in this section is simple to build and may just be the answer to your storage problem. This one was constructed with oak veneer sheet material, but it could be just as easily built with plain MDF or particleboard and painted. I've made mine a little fancier than normal by using solid oak corner and crown moulding. But again, it isn't necessary to spend the extra money if you're looking only for a plain and simple wardrobe. Commercially made wardrobes are somewhat expensive. And if they have a drawer like the one in this project, the price really climbs.

You should save a considerable sum of money by building your own wardrobe. The final cost, however, is dependent on what type of sheet material you decide to use, the size of the wardrobe and the cost of solid-wood trim that might be added.

You can trim out the cabinet using iron-on veneer edge tape, which is easier and much less costly. The only other change would be how the back is installed and the bottom and top boards are joined to the sides. If you have the equipment, use biscuits to join the sides to both bottom and top boards. The back should be set into rabbet cuts on panels A and B and shelf K will have to be reduced in depth by ¼", or the depth of the rabbet cuts, for the back. This alternative building method would be simpler and one that I will consider for my next wardrobe, but the choice is yours.

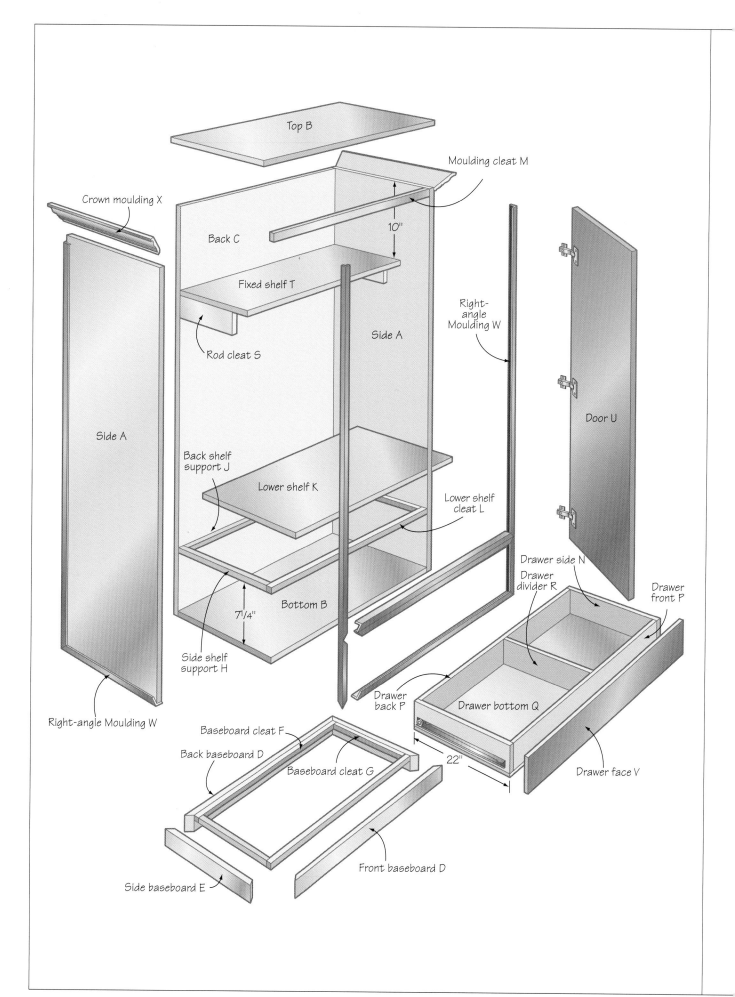

Top B

Moulding cleat M

Crown moulding X

Back C

10"

Right-angle Moulding W

Fixed shelf T

Rod cleat S

Side A

Side A

Door U

Back shelf support J

Lower shelf K

Lower shelf cleat L

Right-angle Moulding W

Bottom B

7¼"

Side shelf support H

Drawer side N

Drawer divider R

Drawer front P

Drawer back P

Drawer bottom Q

Baseboard cleat F

Back baseboard D

22"

Baseboard cleat G

Drawer face V

Front baseboard D

Side baseboard E

REFERENCE	QUANTITY	PART	STOCK	THICKNESS	(mm)	WIDTH	(mm)	LENGTH	(mm)
A	2	sides	veneer PB	$^{11}/_{16}$	(18)	$23^1/_2$	(597)	80	(2032)
B	2	top & bottom	veneer PB	$^{11}/_{16}$	(18)	$23^1/_2$	(597)	$46^5/_8$	(1184)
C	1	back	veneer ply	$^1/_4$	(6)	48	(1219)	80	(2032)
D	2	front & back baseboards	veneer PB	$^{11}/_{16}$	(18)	3	(76)	44	(1118)
E	2	side baseboards	veneer PB	$^{11}/_{16}$	(18)	3	(76)	$19^3/_4$	(502)
F	2	baseboard cleats	hardwood	$^3/_4$	(19)	$^3/_4$	(19)	42	(1067)
G	2	baseboard cleats	hardwood	$^3/_4$	(19)	$^3/_4$	(19)	17	(432)
H	2	side shelf supports	hardwood	$^3/_4$	(19)	$^3/_4$	(19)	$22^3/_4$	(578)
J	1	back shelf support	hardwood	$^3/_4$	(19)	$^3/_4$	(19)	$45^1/_8$	(1146)
K	1	lower shelf	veneer PB	$^{11}/_{16}$	(18)	$23^1/_2$	(597)	$46^5/_8$	(1184)
L	1	lower shelf cleat	veneer PB	$^{11}/_{16}$	(18)	$^3/_4$	(19)	$46^5/_8$	(1184)
M	1	moulding cleat	veneer PB	$^{11}/_{16}$	(18)	$^3/_4$	(19)	$46^5/_8$	(1184)
N	2	drawer sides	Baltic birch	$^1/_2$	(13)	$5^1/_2$	(140)	22	(559)
P	2	drawer front & back	Baltic birch	$^1/_2$	(13)	$5^1/_2$	(140)	$44^5/_8$	(1134)
Q	1	drawer bottom	Baltic birch	$^1/_2$	(13)	22	(559)	$45^5/_8$	(1159)
R	1	drawer divider	Baltic birch	$^1/_2$	(13)	$5^1/_2$	(140)	21	(533)
S	2	rod cleats	hardwood	$^3/_4$	(19)	$3^1/_2$	(89)	14	(356)
T	1	fixed shelf	veneer PB	$^{11}/_{16}$	(18)	16	(406)	$46^5/_8$	(1184)
U	2	doors	veneer PB	$^{11}/_{16}$	(18)	$23^{13}/_{16}$	(605)	70	(1778)
V	1	drawer face	veneer PB	$^{11}/_{16}$	(18)	$8^1/_2$	(216)	$47^3/_4$	(1213)
W		right angle moulding		$^{11}/_{16}$	(18)	$^{11}/_{16}$	(18)	48'	(14.6m)
X		crown moulding				$3^1/_8$	(79)	8'	(2.4m)

6–107° European hidden hinges

3–handles

1 set–22" (559mm) bottom mount drawer glide

1 clothes rod or $1^1/_2$" (38mm) diameter wood dowel

glue

brad nails

2" (51mm) PB screws

finishing nails

$1^1/_4$" (32mm) PB screws

1" (25mm) PB screws

wood buttons

iron-on edge tape

2 Install the $^1/_4$" thick veneer plywood back C. Glue and finishing nails, spaced about 8" apart, will hold the panel securely.

1 Cut the two sides A, as well as the top and bottom B to the sizes detailed in the materials list. Attach the sides to the top and bottom. They should be flush with the ends of each side board. Use glue and five 2" PB screws per joint. Install the screws through the side panels, but be sure to drill pilot holes for the particleboard screws to insure maximum hold.

Calculate, then Cut

The two doors U and one drawer face V can be cut from one sheet of material. Before ripping the door widths, crosscut the drawer face. Calculating door widths when using European hidden hinges is simple. First, measure the inside cabinet, then, add 1" to that dimension and divide by two. That will be the door width.

My doors U and drawer front V are made from $^{11}/_{16}$"-thick veneer particleboard. Cut the two doors and one drawer face. Apply edge tape to all exposed edges before installing.

To install the doors, use three 107° European hidden hinges for each door. The bottom edge of the drawer face V is flush with the lower edge of bottom B. It's attached with four 1"-long screws through the drawer box. Leave a ½" gap between the top edge of the drawer face and bottom edge of the doors.

3 Apply glue to the top of all shelf supports H and J and install the shelf K. It is secured in place with a few finishing nails through the top face and into the supports.

4 Moulding cleat M should be installed on the underside of the top B at this time. Follow the same procedures as detailed in step 5.

5 If you decided to use iron-on veneer edge tape, you can skip this step. The edge trim is right-angle hardwood moulding W. It measures $^{11}/_{16}$" × $^{11}/_{16}$" on the inside faces. The moulding is cut at 45° at all corners. On the lower shelf K and fixed shelf T, the horizontal moulding strips must be trimmed square after the 45° is cut. A straight cut, where the moulding sides meet at the back of the 45°, is needed so it will properly join the vertical moulding strips. Apply corner moulding to the front closet section, as well as the drawer section. The top and shelf trim is installed on the inside of the cabinet while the bottom trim is on the outside. Glue and nail the mouldings to each side. You'll need one strip on the bottom and one on each front and back edge. Stop the moulding $^{11}/_{16}$" from the top to allow room for attaching the crown. The 45° cuts that meet at the outside intersection of the bottom shelf will create a wedge gap. This can be filled by cutting a small wedge and carefully pushing it into the hole. Glue is all that's needed to hold the wedge in place.

6 I've used 3⅛"-high crown moulding X for the top of my wardrobe. Cut the moulding upside down in your miter box to achieve the correct 45° angle. The crown is attached with glue and finishing nails. It should be installed $^{11}/_{16}$" down from the top of each side A.

7. This drawer box, like a few other projects in this book, is made with ½"-thick Baltic birch plywood. Refer to project three in chapter three for details on building this type of drawer box. The corner joints can be butt joined with glue and screws, or the front and back P can be set in ¼"-deep by ½"-wide rabbets in the sides N and secured with glue and brad nails. My drawer calls for a butt joint at each corner, but you can cut a rabbet in the sides and increase the length of each front and back P by ½". However, remember the rule when installing drawer glides. Most manufacturers require ½" clearance per side. It's also good practice to build the drawer box at least 1" less than the available vertical space. I've used 22" bottom-mount drawer glides and added a center divider R in the box for added strength. Baltic birch — or as it's sometimes called, cabinet-grade plywood — is void free. Therefore, the exposed edges can be sanded smooth.

8. Mount the two rod cleats S, 10" down from the top B. Drill pilot holes and attach the cleats with glue and 1¼" screws. Plug the screw head holes with wood buttons.

9. The fixed shelf T is ¹¹⁄₁₆" thick by 16" deep and 46⅝" wide. Apply glue on top of the rod cleats S and secure the shelf T with a few brad nails. This shelf should have its front edge covered with iron-on edge tape. Mount a clothes rod about 12" out from the back. I've used a commercial version that was made from metal.

Construction Options

Dozens of door options are available. However, frame-and-panel models made by a door factory will be expensive because these are large doors. You can build your own frame-and-panel doors as shown in chapter two or the style shown in chapter four. Veneer particleboard doors with taped edges are reasonably priced but very plain looking. If you want something a little fancier without spending a great deal of money, you can add moulding to the door slab.

The corner trim is an option you can eliminate. It's a different treatment and one that requires a fair amount of patience. Simply applying wood veneer edge tape to all exposed edges is an acceptable and less costly alternative, as mentioned at the start of this project.

A 1½"-diameter wood dowel can be used for the hanging rod. But the commercial metal version is adjustable and easy to install. A wide variety of accessories are available for closets nowadays as well, so it would be worth your time to browse through the home store for additional ideas.

Less-expensive sheet goods can be used if you plan to paint the wardrobe. If, for example, you need a clothing storage center in your basement, use ¾" particleboard or MDF. Give the wardrobe a couple of coats of good paint and you'll have a great storage center for all those seasonal clothes.

And finally, the wardrobe can be any size you need to fit your requirements or space allowance. I've got a lot of room available, so mine is 48" wide. However, this project can just as easily be constructed to any size that suits your needs.

window seat

This window bench project would be a welcome addition to any room in your home. Build it for the living room and get extra seating, as well as storage for firewood; the children's room to provide a quiet place to stare out the window and store toys; or use it under a window in your bedroom and take advantage of the added storage for bed linens. This bench would also be a nice furniture accent piece at the foot of your bed.

I will be using my bench in the living room for extra seating and firewood storage, as I mentioned. However, it seems my dog has decided the bench was made for him to watch over his kingdom through our picture window. The cushion makes a great bed, and he's taken control of the bench, so there goes my extra seating solution.

I haven't installed panels on the inside of the box because I won't be storing anything of value. If you plan on using it for bed linens, or any other delicate items, you can install ¼"-thick veneer plywood panels, as I'll detail in the building steps.

I didn't realize how popular this window bench would be until I heard all the positive comments. It seems this project is on everyone's wish list, so I'll have to make a few more for family and friends. It's easy to build and simple to resize, so it can be custom built to meet any requirements.

Pocket hole joinery is perfect for this project. The frame-and-panel design is well suited to this joinery method, and the thick panels add a great deal of strength to the box. It should support a lot of weight.

The cushion is a piece of fabric covering a sheet of soft foam. The cover I used can be removed and washed, because I installed a zipper and purchased a machine-washable fabric. The seat pad is held in place with hook and loop fasteners so it won't move when someone sits down or the top is opened. Small strips of hook and loop fasteners can be purchased in any linen supply store.

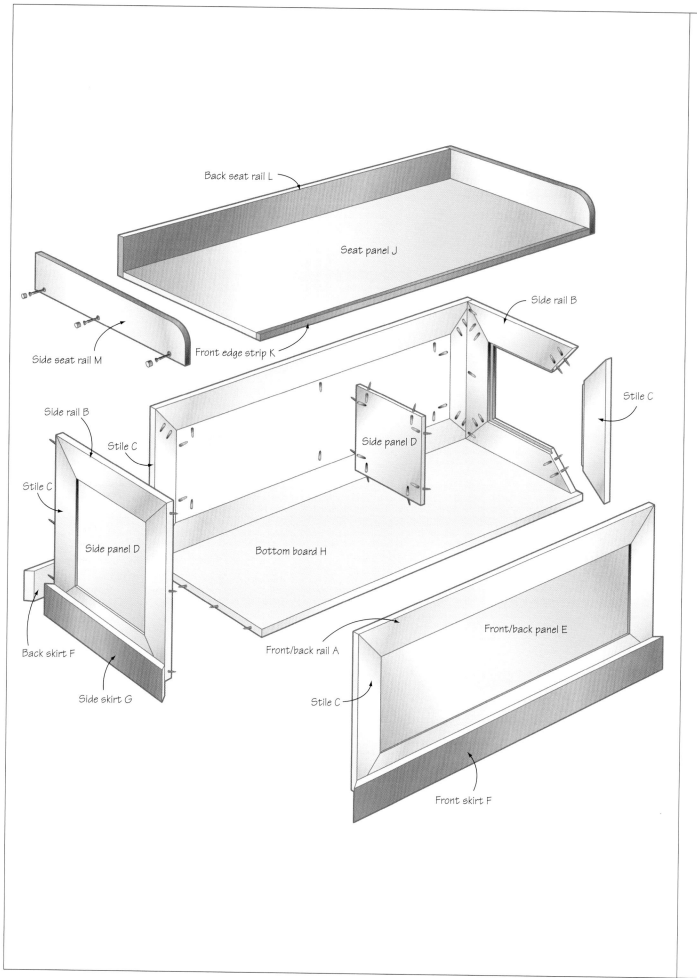

Back seat rail L

Seat panel J

Side rail B

Side seat rail M

Front edge strip K

Stile C

Side rail B

Stile C

Side panel D

Stile C

Side panel D

Bottom board H

Front/back panel E

Back skirt F

Side skirt G

Front/back rail A

Stile C

Front skirt F

REFERENCE	QUANTITY	PART	STOCK	THICKNESS	(mm)	WIDTH	(mm)	LENGTH	(mm)	COMMENTS
A	4	front and back rails	solid wood	³/₄	(19)	3	(76)	43	(1092)	mitered
B	4	side rails	solid wood	³/₄	(19)	3	(76)	15	(381)	mitered
C	8	stiles	solid wood	³/₄	(19)	3	(76)	15	(381)	mitered
D	2	side panels	veneer PB	¹/₂	(13)	10	(254)	10	(254)	
E	2	front and back panels	veneer PB	¹/₂	(13)	10	(254)	38	(965)	
F	2	front and back skirts	solid wood	³/₄	(19)	3	(76)	44¹/₂	(1131)	
G	2	side skirts	solid wood	³/₄	(19)	3	(76)	18	(457)	
H	1	bottom board	particleboard	¹¹/₁₆	(18)	16¹/₂	(419)	43	(1092)	
J	1	seat panel	particleboard	¹¹/₁₆	(18)	17¹/₄	(438)	43¹/₂	(1105)	
K	1	front edge strip	solid wood	¹¹/₁₆	(18)	¹/₂	(13)	43¹/₂	(1105)	
L	1	back seat rail	solid wood	³/₄	(19)	3	(76)	43¹/₂	(1105)	
M	2	side seat rails	solid wood	³/₄	(19)	3	(76)	18¹/₂	(470)	

Note: PB = particleboard.

HARDWARE AND SUPPLIES

Pocket hole screws: 1¹/₄"
(32mm)

Wood screws: 1¹/₄" (32mm),
1¹/₂" (38mm)

PB screws: 2" (51mm)

Brad nails

Glue

3   No-mortise hinges

Wood putty

Wood plugs

Seat fabric

Seat foam

Zipper

Hook and loop fastener strips

1 Cut the four front and back rails A, the four side rails B and the eight stiles C about 1" longer than indicated in the materials list. That extra 1", at this point, will make it easier to machine the rabbets and leave enough room to miter the ends. Note that measurements for all rails and stiles are taken along the longest points of the miters. Next, set your table saw blade to cut a ½"-deep groove along one edge of each board. The outside edge of the cut should be ½" in from a face side.

2 The next cut, on the flat face of each board with the groove ½" from that face, will form a rabbet that's ½" wide by ½" deep. The opposite face will have a ¼"-wide lip remaining.

3   After cutting the rabbets, each board needs a 45° miter on both ends. The rabbet should be along the shortest edge of the mitered boards. Then drill two pocket holes on both ends of each stile C (vertical member). These pocket holes are on the inside (rabbet) face of each stile, as shown.

4   Assemble the four frames, using 1¼"-long pocket hole screws and glue. The front and back frames should measure 15" high by 43" long, and the two side frames should be 15" high by 15" long. Because the pocket holes are closer to the inside edge of the miter, they tend to pull the miter apart on the outside edge. To prevent this, clamp the miters after installing the pocket hole screws and leave them until the adhesive cures.

5   The center panels D and E for the frames are ½"-thick veneer particleboard. These panels are secured with 1¼" pocket hole screws and glue. Two screws on the 10"-long edge and three on the 38"-long edge will hold them securely. Remember to reset your pocket hole drill jig for ½"-thick material.

6   The two end panels are joined to the front and back panels with glue and pocket hole screws. Drill three pocket holes on the vertical edges of each end panel, placing one at each end and one in the center.

7   The base skirt is made using ¾"-thick by 3"-high hardwood. It's attached to the bottom of the side and end panels with glue and 1¼"-long wood screws. The skirt boards are aligned 1" above the bottom edges of the box panels, and each corner is mitered. The measurements for skirt boards F and G are taken at the longest edge of the miter cuts. I used a cove router bit to profile the top, outside edges of my skirt boards.

8   The bottom board H is $^{11}/_{16}$" veneer particleboard. Secure it to the bottom edges of the four panels, using glue and 1½"-long wood screws.

9   The seat panel J is also a piece of $^{11}/_{16}$"-thick veneer particleboard. After installing the front edge strip, side and back rails, the seat will overhang each side by 1", and the front face of the bench by 2". I have aligned it flush with the back face of the box so I can install hinges. Cut the seat board J to the size shown in the materials list, and attach the ½"-thick strip K to the front edge, using glue and brad nails. Fill the nail holes with colored putty that matches your final finish and sand the strip smooth.

10   The back rail L and side rails M will strengthen the seat and hold the cushion in place. The two side rails overlap the ends of the back rail. All seat rails are secured with glue and 2" particleboard screws in counterbored holes that are filled with wood plugs. Before installing the side rails, cut a smooth radius on the front top corners. This will remove the sharp corners and help to prevent injury if someone sits too close to either side rail. The seat rail bottom edges are aligned flush with the bottom face of seat board J.

11   I'm using three no-mortise hinges to attach the seat to the box.

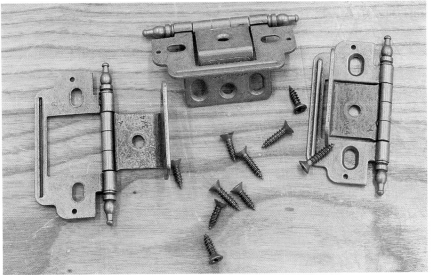

46

chest of drawers

The project in this chapter is a chest of drawers, but again, it's a project that details construction procedures that can be applied to other pieces of furniture. Any type of case or carcass that has drawers can be built following the steps outlined in this chapter. However, this building style is best suited for bedroom chests and dressers.

I am using a combination of oak plywood and particleboard (PB) veneer sheet material. Sheet goods are stable, but the edges can be damaged, particularly in high-use areas such as the bedroom, so the top's perimeter and drawers have hardwood edges applied. This is a common technique that lowers the cost of construction, takes advantage of stable sheet material and gives the woodworker an opportunity to machine or profile the edges because of the applied hardwood.

Another common material is used to build the drawer boxes. Baltic birch, sometimes referred to as cabinet-grade plywood, is a favorite building material with many cabinetmakers. The multilayer colored edges can be sanded smooth and left exposed because of the void-free properties of this material. Baltic birch is reasonably priced, stable and easy to use. Pocket hole screws, nails and glue are used to create strong joints with this material.

I'm taking advantage of modern hardware and using bottom-mounted drawer glides that attach to the cabinet sides and drawer boxes; no additional support frames are required. I'm also building the cabinet in a frameless style, which is an ideal application when low-cost, good-quality and sturdy case goods are required. These frameless-style cabinets may not be destined to become prized antiques, but they will serve you well for many years as good-quality cabinets for any room in your home. They are a cost-effective solution for the guest room or child's bedroom.

This chest of drawers is 30" wide by 48" high and 19" deep. However, you can make it any size you require, and I discuss the options in the Construction Notes at the end of this chapter.

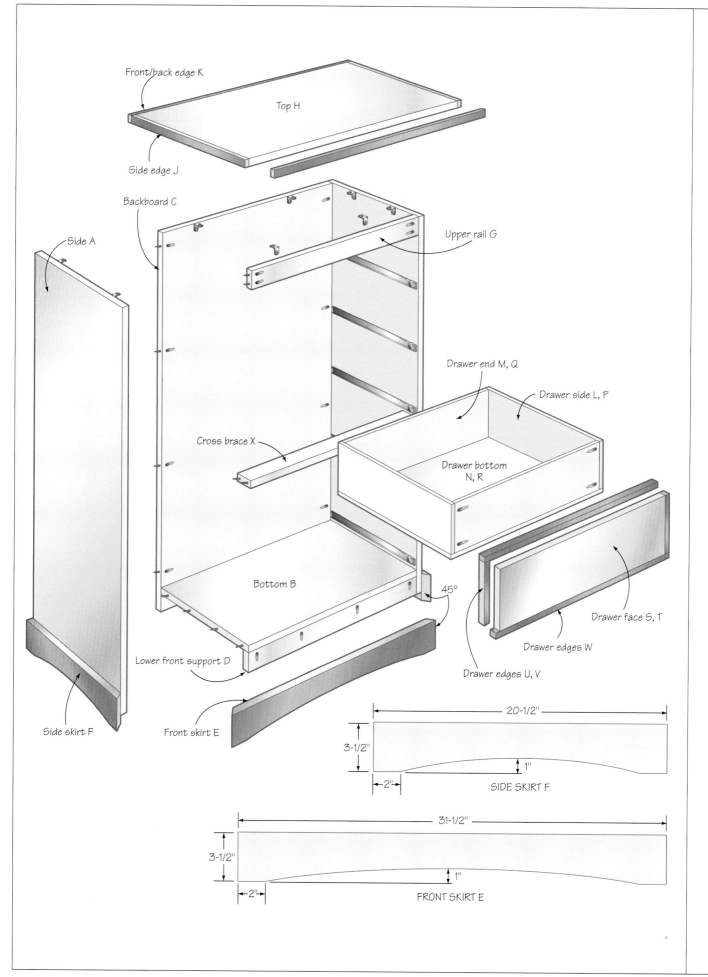

Front/back edge K

Top H

Side edge J

Backboard C

Side A

Upper rail G

Drawer end M, Q

Drawer side L, P

Cross brace X

Drawer bottom
N, R

Bottom B

45°

Drawer face S, T

Lower front support D

Drawer edges W

Side skirt F

Front skirt E

Drawer edges U, V

20-1/2"

3-1/2"

1"

2"

SIDE SKIRT F

31-1/2"

3-1/2"

1"

2"

FRONT SKIRT E

CHEST OF DRAWERS | INCHES (MILLIMETERS)

HARDWARE AND SUPPLIES

Pocket hole screws: 1¼"
(32mm), 1" (25mm)

Wood screws: ⅝" (16mm),
1" (25mm)

Brad nails

Glue

Iron-on wood veneer tape

Right-angle brackets

Wood putty

Drawer glides

Drawer pulls

REFERENCE	QUANTITY	PART	STOCK	THICKNESS	(mm)	WIDTH	(mm)	LENGTH	(mm)
A	2	sides	veneer ply	¾	(19)	19	(483)	46	(1168)
B	1	bottom	veneer ply	¾	(19)	19	(483)	28½	(724)
C	1	backboard	veneer PB	¾	(19)	28½	(724)	43¼	(1098)
D	1	lower front support	veneer ply	¾	(19)	2	(51)	28½	(724)
E	1	front skirt	hardwood	¾	(19)	3½	(89)	31½	(800)
F	2	side skirts	hardwood	¾	(19)	3½	(89)	20½	(521)
G	1	upper rail	hardwood	¾	(19)	1½	(38)	28½	(724)
H	1	top	veneer ply	¾	(19)	19	(483)	31	(787)
J	2	side edges	hardwood	¾	(19)	½	(13)	19	(483)
K	2	front and back edges	hardwood	¾	(19)	½	(13)	32	(813)
L	8	drawer sides	Baltic birch	½	(13)	5	(127)	18	(457)
M	8	drawer ends	Baltic birch	½	(13)	5	(127)	26½	(673)
N	4	drawer bottoms	Baltic birch	½	(13)	18	(457)	27½	(699)
P	2	drawer sides	Baltic birch	½	(13)	8¾	(222)	18	(457)
Q	2	drawer ends	Baltic birch	½	(13)	8¾	(222)	26½	(673)
R	1	drawer bottom	Baltic birch	½	(13)	18	(457)	27½	(699)
S	4	drawer faces	veneer ply	¾	(19)	7	(178)	28¾	(730)
T	1	drawer face	veneer ply	¾	(19)	9¾	(248)	28¾	(730)
U	2	drawer edges	hardwood	¾	(19)	½	(13)	9¾	(248)
V	8	drawer edges	hardwood	¾	(19)	½	(13)	7	(178)
W	10	drawer edges	hardwood	¾	(19)	½	(13)	29¾	(756)
X	1	cross brace	hardwood	¾	(19)	1½	(38)	28½	(724)

1 Cut the two sides A and bottom B as listed in the materials list. Apply iron-on wood veneer tape to the front edges of all three panels. Then drill four pocket holes on each side of the bottom board. The holes are drilled on the underside of panel B.

2 Join the bottom B to the sides A with glue and 1¼" pocket hole screws. Align panel B so its bottom face is 2" above the ends of each side board.

3 Cut the back-board C to the size indicated in the materials list, and drill pocket holes on the inside face of the sides. Install this panel with 1¼" pocket hole screws and glue. Its back face is aligned flush with the back edges of the side and bottom boards.

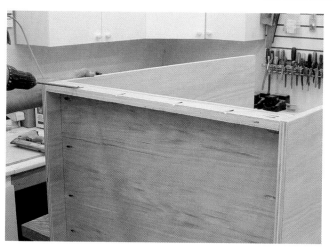

4 The lower front support D is used to strengthen the cabinet base and provide a surface to glue and attach the front skirt board. Install the support board with glue and 1¼" pocket hole screws on the front face, as the skirt board will cover it. Its front face should be flush with the front edges of the side and bottom boards.

5 The front and side skirts E and F are mitered at 45°. They are ¾"-thick hardwood with an arc cut on the lower edge of each piece. Round over the top edges of each piece, using a ⅜"-radius bit in your router, before cutting the miters. These boards are attached to the cabinet carcass with their top edges 2⅛" above the bottom ends of the side and lower support boards. That position will hide the lower front support D to bottom B joint.

6 Before taking the cabinet off your bench, use a ⅜"-radius bit in a router to soften the lower edges of the front and side skirt boards.

Shop Tip

The backboard panel won't be visible, so it can be any ¹¹⁄₁₆"- or ¾"-thick piece of material that you have in your shop. Veneer plywood is expensive, so this is a good place to substitute a less costly material.

7 The upper rail G is attached to the sides with 1¼"-long pocket hole screws and glue on the back face. Align the top edge of this rail with the top edges of the sides A.

8   The top H will be attached to the cabinet using ⅝"-long screws in right-angle metal brackets. Install two brackets on the sides, backboard and back face of the front rail.

9   I will be using a wood edge technique for the cabinet top and drawer faces. Thin strips of ½"-thick wood are attached to all edges with glue and brad nails. As mentioned previously, this technique is a lot less expensive when compared to using solid wood, and it allows the woodworker to profile the panel edges. The top will be 20" deep and 32" wide. The ¾"-thick veneer plywood or PB is 19" deep by 31" wide with ½"-wide strips of hardwood on each edge to achieve the final size. Cut and attach the wood strips J and K. The final size is needed so the top will overhang each side and the front edge of the cabinet by 1", and align flush with the back face.

10   Fill the nail holes with colored putty to match the final finish of your cabinet. Sand the edges and round over the top and bottom face edges of the top with a ⅜"-radius bit. Don't round over the rear, bottom edge, as it will align flush with the back of the cabinet.

Shop Tip

The hardwood skirt board arcs can be cut to the dimensions indicated by using a simple technique. First, drive finishing nails on the waste side of the arc to be cut at the center and both ends. Then, bend a thin strip of hardwood around the nails to form the desired arc. Clamp the ends and trace the arc using the hardwood strip as a guide.

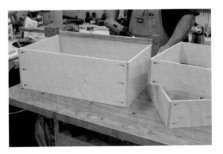

11   Attach the cabinet top, using ⅝"-long wood screws through the brackets. Align the top H with the required overhang as detailed in step 9.

12   Drawer boxes are 1" narrower than the cabinet's interior dimension for most drawer glide hardware. Check the specifications of your hardware before cutting the box parts. The drawer boxes are constructed using ½"-thick Baltic birch plywood. The drawer ends are attached to the drawer sides with 1" pocket hole screws and glue. The bottom drawer box is 27½" wide by 9¼" high, and the four remaining boxes are 27½" wide by 5½" high. All the drawer boxes are 18" deep. Drill the pocket holes, remembering to reset your pocket hole jig for ½" material, and assemble the parts.

Calculating Drawer Box Heights in Frameless Cabinets

This chest of drawers is a frameless-style cabinet with about 41¾" of free space for drawer boxes. Free space is the open area in a cabinet that can be used for drawer boxes.

Generally, drawer boxes require 1" of clearance above and below the box. Between drawer boxes there should be a 2" space, as well as 1" of space above the top box and 1" below the bottom box. However, the bottom box free space can be filled with the cabinet's baseboard because there would be nothing but space and it's not required to remove or operate the drawer box. This is a general rule, and leaves extra room for a little adjusting if required.

This chest of drawers has about 41¾" of open area, which includes a part of the bottom board thickness. I've installed five drawer boxes, which means I need a total of 10" of clearance (2" between each box

and 1" above the top, as well as 1" below the bottom drawer) that can't be used for drawers. Subtract the 10" hardware clearance from the free space height of 41¾" and we are left with 31¾". This remaining space can be occupied by any total height of five drawer boxes. In this project I've reduced the bottom drawer box height by ½" to get a little more space.

Drawer faces can be roughly calculated at a height of 2" greater than the drawer box for material estimation purposes. However, the easiest method is to install the drawer boxes and measure the drawer face heights needed on the cabinet. The drawer height sizes may have to be altered slightly for a visual balance of the faces. After I installed the drawer boxes, I tried a few combinations and arrived at the sizes shown in the material list.

13 Attach the drawer bottoms with glue and brad nails. Align the four panels of each box to the edges of the bottom to square the drawer. If the bottom was cut square, the completed drawer box will be square.

14 The drawer-box bottoms should be aligned at the 0", 11", 19", 27" and 35" marks on the cabinet's interior exposed faces. The measurement begins at the bottom board of the cabinet. A simple way to mark each side panel equally is to use a story stick, as shown. The cabinet runner portions of your drawer glide sets can be attached with ⅝"-long wood screws to the side panels. Be sure to align the drawer runners so the bottom edges of the boxes are at the correct location. The runners should be ⅛" behind the cabinet's front edge.

15 Install the cabinet runners, using a carpenter's square as a guide. The runners should be at a 90° angle to the cabinet's front edge. Attach the drawer-box runners following the manufacturer's specifications and test fit the drawers.

16 The bottom drawer face is 10¾" high, and the remaining four faces are 8" high. They are all 29¾" wide. The drawer faces are made with ¾"-thick veneer plywood or PB. All the edges have a ½"-wide strip of hardwood attached following the same process as the top board. Before installing the drawer faces, round over the front face edges on all the panels.

17 The sides of tall frameless cabinets, such as this chest, could flex if heavy loads were placed in the drawer boxes. To prevent this movement, I install a cross brace after the drawer glide runners are located. It's installed directly under a set of cabinet runners, as close to the middle of the cabinet as possible. The brace won't be seen once the drawer faces are installed. Use glue and two 1¼" pocket hole screws on each end to attach the cross brace X to the cabinet sides.

18 Install the drawer faces with a ⅛" space between each. I always drill my handle or knob holes in the drawer faces and use these holes to drive screws into the box to temporarily secure the face once it has been properly aligned. Then I pull out the drawer, with the face attached, and drive four 1"-long screws through the back side of the front boards and into the rear of the drawer face. Once that is complete, I remove the handle hole screws, drill completely through the box front board and install the drawer handles or knobs.

Construction Notes

This cabinet is more than just a chest of drawers project. It's the basic construction process for all multi-drawer cabinets. The cabinet can be used as a chest of drawers in the bedroom, and a matching dresser can be made following the same steps.

Dressers are much like the chest but are lower and longer. They usually contain two banks of drawers and are about 72" long. When building a dresser, install two center panels at the midpoint of the dresser to support each drawer bank and provide an edge for each of the drawer faces where both meet in the middle.

Wood choice is a matter of personal taste. I used oak veneer plywood and PB because it matches my furniture and it's readily available in this area. The height, width and depth are also a matter of need and design, so any size that suits your requirements is acceptable.

This project illustrated a wood edge technique on the top board and drawer faces. However, they can just as easily be made of solid wood if that's your preference. Solid woods allow more freedom of design, and you might want to profile the edges differently or cut a pattern on each face. The cabinet top can be made to look thicker by using a 1"-high strip of wood for the edge treatment.

The drawer boxes were made using ½"-thick Baltic birch to show that option. However, they can be made with any material, and corners could be joined with dovetails or finger joints if you have the experience. The Baltic birch drawer is a common commercial application for all types of cabinets, including desks and entertainment centers. It's relatively inexpensive and easy to machine.

Design is a matter of personal taste, and the look of any cabinet can be dramatically changed by different trim styles. The skirt boards can be left square or cut with a more complicated pattern. The construction steps are much the same for all drawer bank cabinets, but there are dozens of trim detail possibilities that let you add your personal touch to the cabinets you build.

coffee & end tables

Pocket hole joinery is an ideal application to use when building tables. The skirt-to-leg joint is often made using a mortise-and-tenon joint, but screws in pocket holes, with glue, are another method. The pocket hole system can also be used to secure the tabletops.

This project is another one that deals with the construction process and not necessarily the sizes as detailed. Use the same steps to build a long and low coffee table, or a larger table that can be used as a desk. The variables are the leg lengths and table-top dimensions.

Coffee and end tables become more than just a place to rest cups and glasses with the addition of a drawer. In television or family rooms there's often one or two remote controls, the TV Guide, drink coasters and other small articles that tend to clutter the tabletop surface. The small drawer that's detailed is a great place to store all those items.

End tables normally have the drawer in the end skirt, while long coffee or sofa tables have two drawers in the side skirt. These drawers are simple boxes made with Baltic birch plywood that run on wood cleats. They are simple to build and really add to the usefulness of this piece of furniture.

I built a couple of prototypes before deciding on the final size for my end table. I used some shop scraps to build the models so I could see the finished size in place. My final end table shown here is the perfect size for my sofa, and should be suitable for most applications. A coffee table to match would be lower by about 6" and almost twice as long, at about 48". Your requirements may be slightly different, but end tables that are 19" wide by 26" deep and 22" high, with a matching coffee table at 19" wide by 48" long and 16" high, should suit most rooms.

There are a few material and construction options, which I will discuss in the Construction Notes. However, these tables are always a welcome addition to any room in the home, and you'll likely build more than one set when friends and family see the finished project.

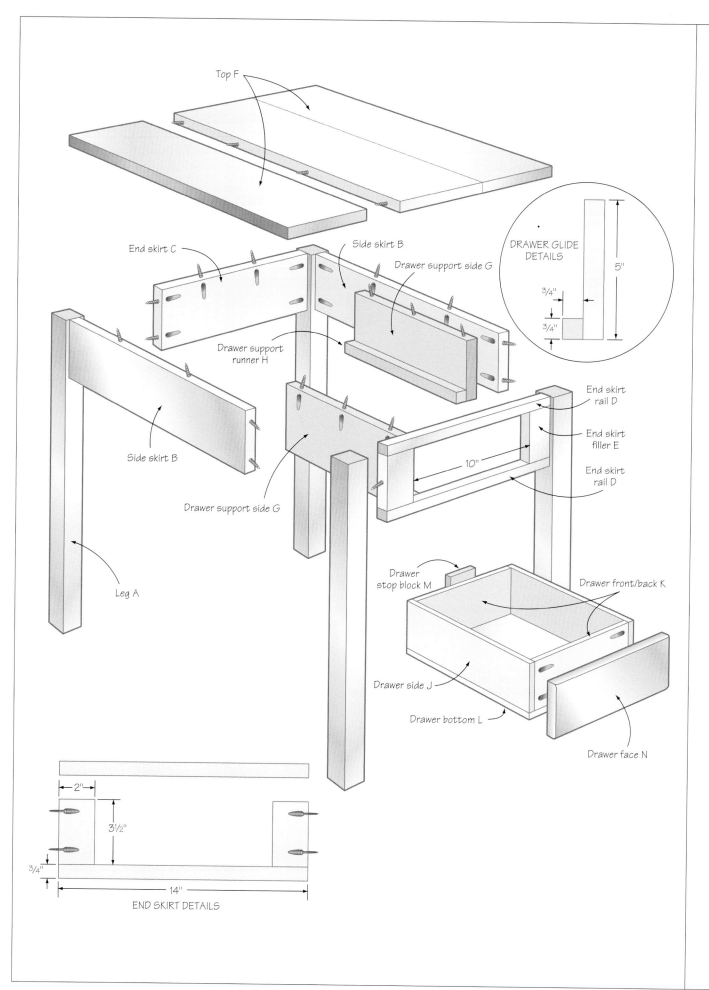

Top F

End skirt C

Side skirt B

Drawer support side G

DRAWER GLIDE
DETAILS

5"

3/4"

3/4"

Drawer support
runner H

End skirt
rail D

End skirt
filler E

Side skirt B

End skirt
rail D

10"

Drawer support side G

Leg A

Drawer
stop block M

Drawer front/back K

Drawer side J

Drawer bottom L

Drawer face N

2"

3½"

3/4"

14"

END SKIRT DETAILS

REFERENCE	QUANTITY	PART	STOCK	THICKNESS	(mm)	WIDTH	(mm)	LENGTH	(mm)
A	4	legs	solid wood	1⅝	(41)	1⅝	(41)	21	(533)
B	2	side skirts	solid wood	¾	(19)	5	(127)	21	(533)
C	1	end skirt	solid wood	¾	(19)	5	(127)	14	(356)
D	2	end skirt rails	solid wood	¾	(19)	¾	(19)	14	(356)
E	2	end skirt fillers	solid wood	¾	(19)	2	(51)	3½	(89)
F	1	top	solid wood	¾	(19)	19¼	(489)	26¼	(666)
G	2	drawer support sides	veneer ply	¾	(19)	5	(127)	12	(305)
H	2	drawer support runners	solid wood	¾	(19)	¾	(19)	12	(305)
J	2	drawer sides	Baltic birch	½	(13)	2⅞	(73)	12	(305)
K	2	drawer back and front	Baltic birch	½	(13)	2⅞	(73)	8⅞	(225)
L	1	drawer bottom	Baltic birch	½	(13)	9⅞	(251)	12	(305)
M	1	drawer stop block	Baltic birch	½	(13)	2	(51)	2	(51)
N	1	drawer face	solid wood	¾	(19)	4½	(115)	11	(279)

HARDWARE AND SUPPLIES

Pocket hole screws: 1¼"
(32mm), 1" (25mm)

Wood screws: 1" (25mm)

Brad nails

Glue

Drawer pull/knob

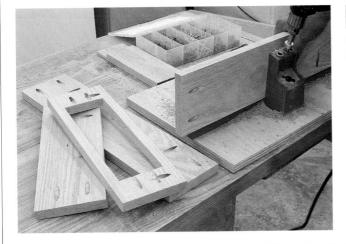

1   Cut the four legs A to the dimensions indicated in the materials list. Use a ⅜"-radius roundover bit to ease the four corners on each leg. The legs are standard 2×2 stock that is normally dressed to 1⅝" by 1⅝" and is available in most lumberyards.

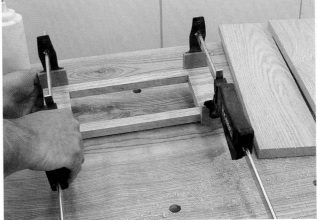

2   Prepare the two sides B and one end skirt C by cutting to size and sanding. The drawer skirt board is made with parts D and E. Assemble as shown in the drawing, using glue and clamps until the adhesive sets. There should be a drawer opening that's 3½" high by 10" wide.

3   Drill pocket holes in each skirt board. Two holes are drilled on each end to attach the boards to the legs. Holes are also required to attach the tabletop, so I drilled two in the long skirt boards and two in the short boards.

4 | The skirt boards are attached to the legs using 1¼" pocket hole screws and glue. If you are building softwood tables, use pocket screws. I have offset the skirt boards by ⅜" behind the face of each leg. Align the top edges of the skirt boards flush with the top ends of each leg. A simple jig with a ⅜"-deep rabbet, as shown in chapter two, is used to equally offset each skirt. The jig can be made on your table saw. A deeper rabbet will set the skirt boards farther back from the leg face, and a shallower groove will move the skirts forward.

5 | The top F is made by gluing up solid-wood boards that are edge joined, glued and secured with 1¼" pocket hole screws. You can dress the edges of each board with a jointer or long-bed hand plane. However, if you don't have access to these tools, you can cut joinable edges on a table saw. To get perfect cuts, be sure the table saw blade is sharp and the fence is accurately aligned to the blade. Cut one edge, then reverse the board, with the first cut edge against the saw fence, and proceed to rip the opposite edge. If the saw is properly aligned, the edges will be parallel to each other and square. Butt the boards together and check the joints. Once the boards butt tightly, drill pocket holes and apply glue to each joined edge. Clamp the top and drive pocket hole screws into the holes to secure the panel. Set aside until the glue sets.

6 | Sand the tabletop smooth, then round over the top and bottom face edges with a ⅜"-radius roundover bit. Before attaching the top, drill the center of each pocket hole with a bit that has a larger diameter than the screw. This larger hole will allow the solid-wood top to move slightly with humidity changes.

7 | Center the table frame on the top with an equal overhang on all legs. Use 1¼" pocket hole screws to attach the top to the frame. Don't use any glue on this joint, so the wood will be free to move if necessary.

8 | Build the two drawer supports with parts G and H. They are secured to the underside of the tabletop with 1¼" pocket-ole screws. Align them so the ¾" by ¾" drawer support runners are flush with the lower skirt rail D. Remember, you can use any scrap material in your shop to build these drawer supports, because they won't be seen.

9   The drawer box tray is made with ½"-thick Baltic birch plywood. It's a very stable sheet material that's commonly used for drawer making. The box is ⅛" narrower and ⅛" lower than the drawer box opening. Cut the parts J, K and L, then secure the back and front boards K to the sides J. The front and back should have two pocket holes drilled on each end, and are attached to the sides with 1"-long pocket hole screws and glue. Remember to set your pocket hole jig drill bit for ½"-thick material.

10   Install the bottom L to the box frame, using glue and brad nails.

11   Install the drawer stop block M on the back of the drawer box. Use glue and brad nails to attach the block, positioning it ½" above the drawer box. This block will prevent the drawer from being pulled all the way out of the drawer opening.

12   The drawer face N is a piece of solid wood with the front face edges rounded over using a ⅜"-radius router bit. Center the drawer face on the box and attach it with 1"-long wood screws through the back face of the

drawer box front board. The table is complete and ready for finishing. I used three coats of satin polyurethane on my table.

Construction Notes

In the introduction to this chapter I discussed the many options available when using these construction steps for various-size tables. A coffee table that's longer and lower is an obvious companion piece to the end table, but a number of other furniture pieces can be built with these techniques. A few to consider might be a bedside table, a small utility side table for the kitchen, a tall narrow table that's typically placed behind a sofa, a writing table or a child's desk. The variations are endless because the leg and skirt construction style is used to build many different pieces of furniture.

I used oak hardwood, but any type of wood can be used. The 5"-high skirt board is a well-proportioned size for these tables, but a 6" board can also be used if you need a deeper drawer box. Thinner legs will make the table appear lighter, and can be used to match your home furnishings. A thicker 1" or 1¼" top dramatically changes the look of these tables, and would be suitable with country-style furniture.

Always secure both pieces tightly before joining, to prevent stripping the screws. Use good-quality glue and the proper screw length for each joint. Use caution when driving the screws, because a stripped thread won't provide a great deal of holding power. And with this project in particular, be sure to correctly align the top edges of the skirt boards with the top of the legs.

sideboard

I originally named this project the kitchen display and storage cabinet. It's ideal as a sideboard and added storage center in a large kitchen, as I originally intended, but it can also be a useful piece of furniture in a small dining room. The center can be used as an addition to your existing buffet and hutch, or as the primary cabinet when space is at a premium.

Someone suggested that it would be a great refreshment storage and service cabinet for the family room. And another person said they'd use it for a basement apartment eat-in kitchen they were building in their home. I had all kinds of suggested uses, which tells me a great deal about the usefulness of this project.

The angled breakfront on the base is a feature that really makes this a unique piece. The cabinet appears to be complex, requiring complicated construction techniques, but is surprisingly simple to build thanks to pocket hole joinery. Traditional angle joinery requires that each part be half the final angle to form the joint. Pocket hole joinery, on the other hand, uses one straight member and a full-angle cut on the joining piece to achieve the required angle.

This unique joining method puts the intersection of both pieces slightly off the angled point, where the joint turns, leaving a crisp corner seam. The line where both pieces are joined is on a flat surface, and not the point, so the joint virtually disappears. It's a lot of fun to experiment with these angled joints using pocket hole joinery, and it opens up a lot of interesting possibilities.

I've done a bit of experimenting with different pocket hole applications in this project, so check out all the techniques and pick a few that work best for you. A note of caution though — this isn't an inexpensive project! The cost of hardwood, veneer plywood, hardware and glass add up quickly, and spending upwards of $300 isn't out of the question. However, you would have difficulty finding a store-bought piece, similar in quality to this project, at that price.

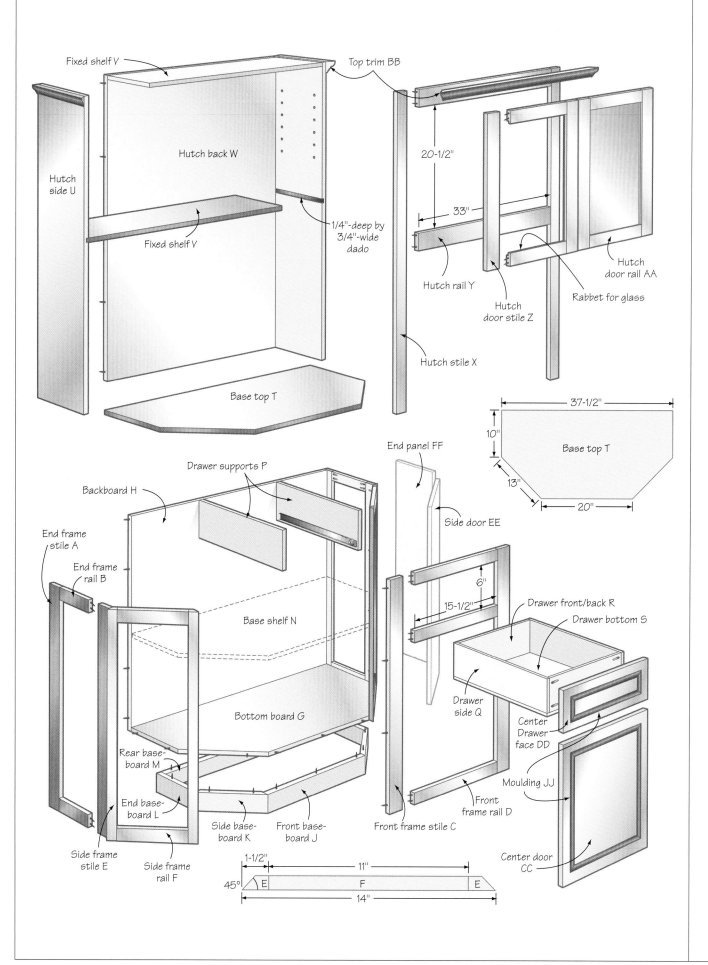

Fixed shelf V

Top trim BB

Hutch back W

Hutch side U

Fixed shelf V

1/4"-deep by 3/4"-wide dado

Base top T

20-1/2"

33"

Hutch rail Y

Hutch door stile Z

Rabbet for glass

Hutch door rail AA

Hutch stile X

37-1/2"

10"

Base top T

13"

20"

End panel FF

Side door EE

Drawer supports P

Backboard H

End frame stile A

End frame rail B

Base shelf N

Drawer front/back R

Drawer bottom S

Drawer side Q

Center Drawer face DD

Bottom board G

Rear base-board M

End base-board L

Side frame stile E

Side frame rail F

Side base-board K

Front base-board J

Front frame stile C

Front frame rail D

Front frame stile C

Moulding JJ

Center door CC

1-1/2"

11"

45° E

F

E

14"

REFERENCE	QUANTITY	PART	STOCK	THICKNESS	(mm)	WIDTH	(mm)	LENGTH	(mm)	COMMENTS
A	4	end frame stiles	hardwood	3/4	(19)	1 1/2	(38)	30	(762)	
B	4	end frame rails	hardwood	3/4	(19)	1 1/2	(38)	7	(178)	
C	2	front frame stiles	hardwood	3/4	(19)	2 1/4	(57)	30	(762)	
D	3	front frame rails	hardwood	3/4	(19)	1 1/2	(38)	15 1/2	(394)	
E	4	side frame stiles	hardwood	3/4	(19)	1 1/2	(38)	30	(762)	angled
F	4	side frame rails	hardwood	3/4	(19)	1 1/2	(38)	11	(279)	
G	1	bottom board	veneer ply	3/4	(19)	18	(457)	37 1/2	(953)	
H	1	backboard	veneer ply	3/4	(19)	30	(762)	37 1/2	(953)	
J	1	front baseboard	veneer ply	3/4	(19)	4	(102)	19	(483)	
K	2	side baseboards	veneer ply	3/4	(19)	4	(102)	11 1/4	(285)	
L	2	end baseboards	veneer ply	3/4	(19)	4	(102)	7 1/2	(191)	
M	1	rear baseboard	veneer ply	3/4	(19)	4	(102)	33 3/4	(857)	
N	1	base shelf	veneer ply	3/4	(19)	17 7/8	(454)	37 3/8	(950)	angled
P	2	drawer supports	veneer ply	3/4	(19)	7 1/2	(191)	18	(457)	
Q	2	drawer sides	Baltic birch ply	1/2	(13)	4 1/2	(115)	18	(457)	
R	2	drawer back and front	Baltic birch ply	1/2	(13)	4 1/2	(115)	13 1/2	(343)	
S	1	drawer bottom	Baltic birch ply	1/2	(13)	14 1/2	(369)	18	(457)	
T	1	base top	hardwood	3/4	(19)	20 1/2	(521)	41	(1041)	angled
U	2	hutch sides	veneer ply	3/4	(19)	9 1/4	(235)	42	(1067)	
V	2	hutch fixed shelves	veneer ply	3/4	(19)	8 1/2	(216)	35	(889)	
W	1	hutch back	veneer ply	3/4	(19)	34 1/2	(877)	42	(1067)	
X	2	hutch stiles	hardwood	3/4	(19)	1 1/2	(38)	42	(1067)	
Y	2	hutch rails	hardwood	3/4	(19)	3 1/2	(89)	33	(838)	
Z	4	hutch door stiles	hardwood	3/4	(19)	2 1/4	(57)	22	(559)	
AA	4	hutch door rails	hardwood	3/4	(19)	2 1/4	(57)	12 1/2	(318)	
BB		top trim	hardwood					6'	(2m)	
CC	1	center door	veneer ply	3/4	(19)	16 1/2	(419)	21 1/2	(546)	
DD	1	center drawer face	veneer ply	3/4	(19)	16 1/2	(419)	7 1/2	(191)	
EE	2	side doors	veneer ply	3/4	(19)	12	(305)	29 1/2	(750)	
FF	2	end panels	veneer ply	3/4	(19)	8	(203)	29 1/2	(750)	
GG	2	hutch door panels	glass	1/8	(3)	13 1/8	(333)	18 1/8	(460)	
HH	1	hutch shelf	glass	1/4	(6)	8 1/4	(209)	34 3/8	(874)	
JJ		moulding						40'	(12m)	cut to fit doors and panels

HARDWARE AND SUPPLIES

Pocket hole screws: 1 1/4" (32mm), 1 1/4" (32mm), 1" (25mm)

Wood screws: 2" (51mm), 5/8" (16mm), 1" (25mm), 1 1/4" (32mm)

Brad nails

Finishing nails

Glue

Shelf pins

Wood veneer edge tape

18" (457mm) full-extension drawer glides

Right-angle metal brackets

Wood putty

Pocket hole plugs

Glass clips

10" (254mm) door hinges

Handles

Cabinet lights

1 | Begin the project by constructing the face frames. The two 10"-wide by 30"-high end frames are built with parts A and B. Use glue and two 1¼" hardwood pocket hole screws at each joint.

2 | The single front frame is built with the 2¼"-wide stiles C and the 1½"-wide rails D. The extra stile width is required to conceal the pocket holes that are drilled on the rear faces to join the middle frame to the side frames. A third rail is installed in this frame, leaving a 6"-high opening below the top rail for the drawer box. Assemble this 20"-wide by 30"-high front frame with two 1¼" pocket hole screws and glue at each joint.

3 | The two side frames require 45° cuts on the outside edges of all stiles. The front faces of the four stiles E, after ripping the angles, are 1½" wide. Unlike traditional joinery, a 45° joint using pocket holes is achieved by cutting the full angle on only one of the pieces to be joined. Join the rails F to the angled stiles E with glue and 1¼" pocket hole screws to form two side frames that are 14" wide, measured on the front face, by 30" high.

4 | Before joining the frames, two drilling steps are needed. First, a column of adjustable shelf pin holes should be drilled. The holes are located on the back faces of the two forward stiles on both end frames, and the back faces of each front frame stile. I'm using a shop-made jig, which is built using a flat steel bar with equally spaced drilled holes and a plywood base with hardwood supports.

5 | Drill pocket holes in the forward stile (stile closest to the cabinet front) on each end frame. These will be used to join the end frames to the side frames. Four holes in each stile will be enough to secure the frames. Pocket holes on the back face of these 1½"-wide stiles will partially tear the edge. However, fixed end panels will hide the tears.

7 Remove the excess angled rip material on the side frames, using a plane or belt sander. Sand all the front faces smooth before proceeding.

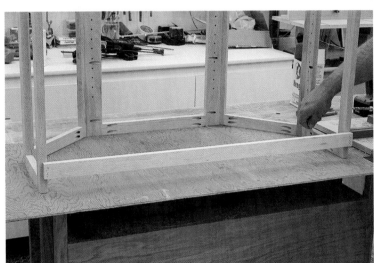

6 Drill four pocket holes on both rear faces of the front frame stiles. They will be used to join the front frame to the two side frames. Join the five frames with glue and 1¼" pocket hole screws. All the back faces of the stiles should be in line at the outside corners. A small part of the 45° angled rip on the side frame stiles will extend past the faces of the end and middle frames. This excess will be removed in the next step.

8 Block the frame by attaching a temporary strap to the back edges of the end frames. Check that all frame-to-frame joints are at 45°. If not, use clamps and wedges cut at 45° to hold the frame in its proper position. The end frames should also be parallel to each other. My inside frame-to-frame dimension is 37½", which may be slightly different from yours, due to cutting and assembly procedures. Create a template of the inside perimeter of the frame, using a thin sheet of plywood or hardboard, and cut it to size. The template will be used to lay out the bottom board G, base shelf N and top T.

9 Use the template to mark the bottom board G. The depth (front to back edge) of the bottom is shortened by ¾" to leave room for the backboard H. Drill pocket holes on the underside of the bottom board for screws that will secure it to the face-frame assembly. The bottom board is attached with 1¼" pocket hole screws and glue, and has its bottom edge aligned flush with the bottom edges of the face frames.

10 The backboard H is also ¾"-thick veneer plywood. Before installing, drill two columns of shelf pin holes in the front face that are aligned with the previously drilled holes in the stiles. The hole columns are located about 10" from each end of this panel. The backboard overlaps the bottom board and is secured with glue and 2" wood screws. Pocket holes on the rear face are used to attach it to each stile of the back frames.

11　The base frame is constructed using ¾"-thick veneer plywood with parts J, K, L and M. All corners are mitered at 45° by cutting each part at 22½°, with the exception of the rear baseboard M, which is a straight butt joint. Drill pocket holes on the inside face of each board and secure them to the bottom board with 1¼" pocket hole screws and glue. Use glue and brad nails at each miter to keep the intersecting joints tight. The frame members are set 2" back from the cabinet face on all edges, including the back face. This 2" setback will provide toe room at the front and sides, and allow the cabinet to rest tight to the wall at the back, because it will be higher than standard wall base trim.

12　Use the template to draw an outline on ¾" veneer plywood for an adjustable base shelf N. It should be reduced by ¹⁄₁₆" on the end, side and front edges, as well as a ¾" reduction on the back edge, so it can be moved easily in the cabinet. Apply iron-on heat-sensitive adhesive wood veneer tape to the end, side and front edges of this shelf board.

13　Cut the two drawer supports P. They are attached to the back faces of the middle frame stiles and the backboard. Use 1¼" pocket hole screws and glue on the front ends and wood screws through the backboard at the rear. Carefully align these support panels so they are flush with the inside edges of the middle frame stiles at the drawer opening. The supports must be parallel to each other and at 90° on the backboard. Use a carpenter's square to draw position lines on the backboard.

14　The drawer box opening is 6" high by 15½" wide and 18¾" deep, so I will build an 18"-deep drawer box. The drawer box is 1" narrower than the opening, and 1" less in height to accommodate the full-extension side-mounted glides that I used. The box is made using ½"-thick Baltic birch, sometimes referred to as cabinet-grade plywood. The sides Q are joined to the front and back R with 1" pocket hole screws and glue. The bottom S is secured with glue and brad nails. The overall dimension of the drawer box is 5" high by 14½" wide and 18" deep.

15 | Install the drawer glides following the manufacturer's instructions. As mentioned, I'm using full-extension glides, but standard, less-expensive three-quarter-extension drawer glides can be used.

16 | The top T is made using solid wood by gluing up a series of ¾"-thick boards. Join the boards using pocket hole joinery and glue. But pay special attention to the placement of the pocket holes, because the top will be cut using the template as a guide. The boards can be edge dressed on a jointer or cut parallel on a well-tuned table saw. If you don't have the equipment, have your lumber supplier dress the edges on their jointer. The charges at most lumberyards for this service are usually reasonable. Once the adhesive has set, cut the top using the template, but add 1" to the ends, sides and front edges. The back is cut to the template dimension so that edge will be flush with the back edge of the cabinet.

17 | The top is secured to the cabinet using right-angle metal brackets and ⅝"-long wood screws. I made the holes in these brackets larger to allow some room for expansion and contraction of the solid-wood top. The enlarged holes are twice the diameter of the screw shaft that I used. Round over the top and bottom edges of the top, using a ¼"-radius roundover bit in a router, but leave the back edge square. Attach the top so there's a 1" overhang on all faces of the cabinet and it is flush with the outside face of the backboard.

18 | The two hutch sides U are ¾"-thick veneer plywood. Drill adjustable shelf pin holes in the top 20" of each side panel, because the upper section will have a fixed shelf at the 24" mark. Keep the rear column of holes 2" away from the back edge of each side to leave room for the ¾"-thick hutch back.

19 | Use a router with a straight-cutting bit or a table saw with a dado blade to cut a ¾"-wide rabbet on the top edge of both side boards. The same setup can be used to cut a ¾"-wide dado on the inside face of each board. These dadoes are 24" below the top edge of each side, measured to the top edge of the dado cut. Both rabbets and dadoes are ¼" deep. If you're using a router, clamp the two sides together to ensure the cuts will be perfectly aligned.

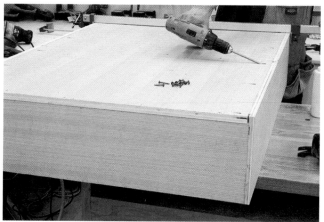

20 The hutch is 36" wide, measured on the outside faces. Two fixed ¾"-thick veneer plywood shelves V are installed in the rabbets and dadoes and secured with glue. Clamp the assembly until the glue sets. The shelves V are ¾" narrower than the sides U. They are installed flush with the front edges of the sides U to leave a ¾"-wide space at the rear for the back.

21 Cut the hutch back W and drill a column of shelf pin holes at the center point to align with the holes in the side boards. The back is attached to the sides using 1¼" pocket hole screws, and to the fixed shelves with 2"-long wood screws and glue on all edges. This full-thickness back will add strength and weight to the hutch, as well as square up the carcass.

22 The hutch face frame is built using 1½"-wide stiles X and 3½"-wide rails Y. Both rail top edges are aligned flush with the upper surfaces of the two fixed shelves. These wide rails will be used to hide light fixtures in the upper and lower sections of the hutch. Attach the rails to the stiles with 1¼" pocket hole screws on the rear face of both rails.

23 Attach the face frame to the hutch carcass with glue and finishing nails. Fill the nail holes with colored putty that matches the cabinet's final finish color. If you prefer, you can attach the face frame using biscuit joinery if you have the equipment.

24 Purchase the top trim moulding BB at this point and mark its position on the cabinet. Use a ¼"-radius roundover bit in a router and ease the outside edges of each stile up to the lower edge of the top trim. Leave the area under the trim moulding square, so it will rest flat on the cabinet frame. Round over the inside edges of the lower section stiles and rails, using the same bit.

Shop Tip

I'm using standard 107° hidden hinges with a special plate. Standard hinge plates are typically attached to the cabinet side board. However, this hutch carcass has a face frame that extends past the inside face of the side boards, meaning a standard plate cannot be installed. A special face-frame mounting plate is used for this application, and is attached to the inside edges of each stile, using ⅝"- or ¾"-long wood screws.

25 The upper opening is 33" wide by 20½" high. The doors will be a frame style with tempered glass center panels. They will be mounted using European hidden hinges and face-frame mounting plates. To calculate the width of each door, add 1" to the opening width and divide by two. Using that formula means I will need two 17"-wide doors (33" + 1" = 34" divided by 2). They will be 22" high to provide a ¾" overlap on the upper and lower rails. The doors are made using 2¼"-wide stiles Z and 2¼"-wide rails AA. They are joined with two 1¼" pocket hole screws and glue at each corner. Drill these pocket holes about ⅛" deeper than standard, as we will be filling them with wood plugs. Keep the pocket holes together and as close to the outside edge as possible to provide room for a rabbet cut that will hold the center tempered glass panel.

26 Fill the pocket holes with wood plugs that match the wood type you are using. Round over the front inner and outer perimeter, using a ¼"-radius router bit.

27 Use a rabbeting bit in your router to form a ⅛"-deep cut on the inside back perimeter of the frame for the tempered glass panel GG. Square the corners and order the size of tempered glass required to fit your rabbet cut. Use small plastic clips and ⅝"-long wood screws to hold the glass securely.

29 The base center door CC, center drawer face DD, two side doors EE and two end panels FF are made using ¾"-thick veneer plywood. All the panel edges have wood veneer tape applied, and the front face has decorative moulding JJ that's 1" in from each edge. This thin decorative moulding adds visual interest to the plain, flat panel, but still lets you build a reasonably priced door. The moulding is glued and nailed in place, and all corners are mitered.

28 Drill two 35mm-diameter hinge holes on the back face of each door, 4" on center from each end. The holes are ⅛" back from the edge of the door. Clamp a straight-edged board in place to align the doors ¾" below the top edge of the lower rail. Secure the hinges in the drilled holes on each door and attach the mounting plates to the hinges. Hold the door in its normally open position and drive ⅝" wood screws through the hinge plate holes and into the stile edges to install the door.

30 Attach the two 8"-wide end panels FF to the base using 1¼"-long wood screws. The screws are driven through the rear face of the rails and into the back of each panel. All doors and these end panels are aligned flush with the bottom end of the lower cabinet rails.

| 31 | Install the two side doors EE and center door CC, using standard 100°–120° hidden hinges and face-frame mounting plates.

| 32 | Attach the drawer face DD with two 1"-long wood screws driven through the front board of the drawer box and into the back of the drawer face. There should be a ½" space between the top of the center door and bottom edge of the drawer face. The easiest way to accurately locate the drawer face is to drill the handle holes only in the face. Then, align the door and drive screws through the handle holes and into the drawer box to temporarily secure the face. Gently open the drawer and install two 1¼"-long wood screws through the drawer box. Remove the screw from the handle hole, complete the drilling, then install your handle hardware after the cabinet has been finished.

Construction Notes

Attach the top trim moulding BB, order the door and tempered shelf glass and apply the finish. Your tempered center panel door glass may be slightly different in size from mine, as it depends on the width of cut from your rabbeting bit.

Panels FF are fixed in place on my cabinet, but they can be mounted on hinges if you have easy access to both ends. You might also want to add a pullout shelf on full-extension drawer glides behind the center door for easier access to goods stored in the cabinet.

I mentioned some of the suggestions about different uses for this cabinet in the introduction. They were all valid and I'm sure there are many more applications for this versatile storage center. Don't feel restricted, however, by the sizes I used for this project. The base and hutch can be any size, and the calculations are reasonably straightforward. The base center frame can be any width. For example, if I wanted a 60"-wide base, I would increase the width of the center frame by 21", and the template would follow the new frame assembly width. The hutch backboard, top and bottom fixed shelves, rail and so on, would all have to be wider. Simply put, you can customize the cabinet size to fit your requirements.

I used flat panel doors with a little moulding, but any door style that suits your décor is fine. Once again, I built the cabinet using red oak, but you can use any wood you prefer. As I continue to say, my dimensions and designs are only suggestions, so I urge you to experiment with materials and sizes if your requirements are different from mine.

china hutch

I built this cabinet to be installed in an eating area off the kitchen, next to a family room. Since space was an issue in this high traffic area, the cabinet is 12" deep. However, if you're lucky enough to have a lot of space, the base depth can be easily increased. Remember though, if you do build the 12"-deep version, anchor the cabinet to the wall studs.

The lower section of the cabinet is used to store bowls, fondue pots and other specialized cookware. It's accessible so when Aunt Sarah comes to visit you can easily find that strange bowl she gave you as a wedding present. The top section, behind glass doors, features two glass shelves that are ideal for showing off crystal and glassware. And the round side shelves are perfect for displaying collectibles.

I also installed three fluorescent light fixtures; one on top, another in the upper section and the third behind the wide rail above the base top. I located a three-lever switch that fits into a single electrical box and mounted it behind the upper cabinet bottom rail. The beautiful collection of teapots and glassware shown in this cabinet is owned by Peter and Elaine Marr of Russell, Ontario.

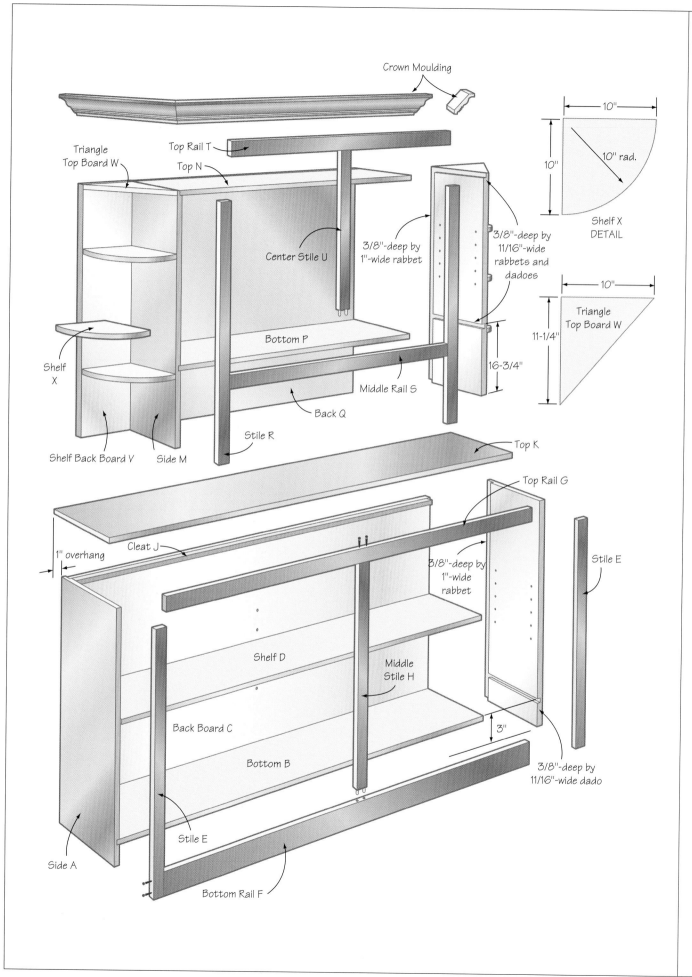

Crown Moulding

Triangle Top Board W

Top Rail T

Top N

Center Stile U

3/8"-deep by 1"-wide rabbet

3/8"-deep by 11/16"-wide rabbets and dadoes

Shelf X DETAIL

10"

10"

10" rad.

Bottom P

Middle Rail S

16-3/4"

Back Q

Stile R

Shelf X

Shelf Back Board V

Side M

10"

Triangle Top Board W

11-1/4"

Top K

Top Rail G

Cleat J

1" overhang

Stile E

3/8"-deep by 1"-wide rabbet

Shelf D

Middle Stile H

Back Board C

Bottom B

3"

Side A

Stile E

3/8"-deep by 11/16"-wide dado

Bottom Rail F

REFERENCE	QUANTITY	PART	STOCK	THICKNESS	(mm)	WIDTH	(mm)	LENGTH	(mm)	COMMENTS
A	2	sides	oak PB	11/16	(18)	11 1/4	(285)	34	(864)	
B	1	bottom	oak PB	11/16	(18)	10 1/2	(267)	71 3/8	(1813)	
C	1	back board	oak PB	11/16	(18)	34	(864)	71 3/8	(1813)	
D	2	shelves	oak PB	11/16	(18)	10 1/8	(257)	70 1/2	(1791)	
E	2	stiles	oak	3/4	(19)	1 1/2	(38)	34	(864)	
F	1	bottom rail	oak	3/4	(19)	3	(76)	69	(1756)	
G	1	top rail	oak	3/4	(19)	1 1/2	(38)	69	(1756)	
H	1	middle stile	oak	3/4	(19)	1 1/2	(38)	29 1/2	(750)	
J	1	cleat	oak	3/4	(19)	1	(25)	70 3/8	(1788)	
K	1	top	oak	3/4	(19)	13	(330)	74	(1880)	
L	4	doors	oak	3/4	(19)	17 3/8	(442)	31	(787)	
	8	107° european hinges								
HUTCH										
M	2	sides	oak PB	11/16	(18)	11 1/4	(285)	46	(1168)	
N	1	top	oak PB	11/16	(18)	10 1/4	(260)	51 3/8	(1305)	
P	1	bottom	oak PB	11/16	(18)	10 1/4	(260)	51 3/8	(1305)	
Q	1	back	oak PB	11/16	(18)	46	(1168)	51 3/8	(1305)	
R	2	stiles	oak	3/4	(19)	1 1/2	(38)	46	(1168)	
S	1	middle rail	oak	3/4	(19)	3	(76)	49	(1245)	
T	1	top rail	oak	3/4	(19)	3	(76)	49	(1245)	
U	1	center stile	oak	3/4	(19)	1 1/2	(38)	26 3/8	(670)	
V	2	shelf back boards	oak	3/4	(19)	10	(254)	46	(1168)	
W	2	triangle top boards	oak	3/4	(19)	10	(254)	11 1/8	(282)	
X	6	shelves	oak	3/4	(19)	10	(254)	10	(254)	with a radius front
Y	4	doors	oak	3/4	(19)	12 3/8	(315)	28 1/2	(724)	
		3' of 3 1/4" crown moulding								
	8	107° european hinges								

Note: PB = particleboard.

HARDWARE AND SUPPLIES

Pocket hole screws: 1 1/4" (32mm)

Wood screws: 1 1/4" (32mm), 1 1/2" (38mm)

PB screws: 2" (51mm)

Brad nails

Glue

3 No-mortise hinges

Wood putty

Wood plugs

Seat fabric

Seat foam

Zipper

Hook and loop fastener strips

1 Prepare the two side panels A as shown in the Materials List. Cut an 11/16"-wide by 3/8"-deep dado, 3" up from the bottom edge in each panel. Note that the back board rabbets are cut 1" wide and 3/8" deep to accept an 11/16"-thick back board. As you know, most walls aren't straight so it's difficult to tightly fit a wide, flat back board. The extended side panels usually make it easier to get a tight fit.

2 Cut and install the bottom board B. Secure it in the dadoes with glue, and clamp tightly or nail from the outside of the side panels. Use two 2½" finishing nails per side; sink the nail heads and fill the holes with colored putty.

3 Place the back board C in the side rabbets and secure using glue and 2½" finishing nails from the back. The thick back board serves three purposes. First, it adds weight to the shallow base. Secondly, it supports the bottom fixed shelf using glue and 2" screws 6" apart through the back board. And third, the board is thick enough to accept holes for the adjustable shelf pins which will provide the necessary support for the long shelves

4 Install the two outside stiles E using glue and face nail with 2½" finishing nails. Fill the nail holes with colored putty. The stiles are attached flush with the outside edges of the credenza sides. If you prefer, the stiles can be attached with glue and biscuits.

Tip

It's common to tear the veneer when cross-grain cutting with a dado blade in your table saw. To prevent this, cut through the veneer with a sharp knife before using the table saw. A router gives the cleanest cut, but use carbide-tipped bits because of the high glue content in particleboard.

5   The bottom rail F is glued and nailed flush with the top surface of the bottom board. Drill and counterbore two holes in the edge of each stile. Secure the stiles to the bottom rail with glue and 2" wood screws. The counterbored holes are filled with ⅜" wood plugs. The top rail G is also secured with glue and two 2" screws through the stiles, then the holes are filled with wood plugs. Its top edge is flush with the stiles' top ends. This rail will be strengthened when it's screwed into the credenza top board.

6   The middle stile H is attached to the bottom rail with glue and two ⅜" dowels. The top end is secured with 2" wood screws through the top edge of the top rail. Install the stile so there is equal spacing on both sides.

7   Drill holes for the adjustable shelf pins. I used ⅜"-diameter brass shelf pins, spaced 2" apart. There are two columns of holes in each side panel, one column in the middle of the back board and another on the inside face of the middle stile. Use a piece of scrap wood to make a jig for the shelf holes. Cut the two shelves D for the base section, then apply wood veneer tape to the front edge of each shelf. Now is an ideal time to fill any nail holes, sand the cabinet and round over the outside edges of the stiles with a ⅜" router bit.

8   Cut and secure the wood cleat J flush with the top inside edge of the back board. Use glue and 1¼" screws to fasten the cleat.

Construction Notes

For this project I purchased ready-made cathedral oak doors. I used standard 107° full-overlay European hidden hinges with face-frame style mounting plates. Drill the 35mm holes in the doors and install the hinges as detailed by the manufacturer.

There are many options when doors are being considered. The simplest method, which doesn't involve any tools, is to purchase doors from a supplier. They are reasonably priced, and there are dozens of door factories looking for your business.

If you want to explore the whole range of door options, take a look at my book, Building Cabinet Doors and Drawers.

9 | Glue up ¾"-thick boards to form a top K that's 13" deep and 74" wide. Glue-ups are best accomplished using biscuit joinery, although a simple edge glue joint will be fine for this application. Slightly ease the two front corners of the top with a belt sander to eliminate the sharp corners. Round over the top and bottom, front and side edges with a ⅜" roundover bit in a router. Drill pilot holes in the cleat J and top rail G for screws that will secure the top. Attach the top using 2" wood screws, making sure there is a 1" overhang on the front edge and at each end. The screws are installed from the underside of the cleat and top rail into the top. I spaced my screws 12" apart. Don't use any glue, and run the drill bit from side to side in the cleat and top rail to make the screw holes larger. This will let the solid wood top move when it expands and contracts with humidity changes.

10 | Cut the two upper side panels M as shown in the Materials List, then cut the ⅜"-deep dadoes and rabbets as detailed in the illustration. Note that the rabbet for the back board is cut 1" wide to accept an ¹¹/₁₆"-thick panel. This leaves enough room to route the lighting wires behind the back board. The top N and bottom P can be glued and clamped into the dadoes and rabbets. The top board can be nailed from the outside edge of the side because a board will be installed over the nail heads.

11 Secure the back board Q to the cabinet, in the rabbets, with glue and finishing nails. Drive the nails through the back board into the cabinet sides at a slight angle and set the nail heads. The back board is attached flush with the top edge of the cabinet side boards.

12 Glue and face nail the two outside stiles R flush with the outside face of the cabinet side boards. Again, use biscuits to attach the stiles if you prefer. Cut the middle rail S to length and attach it to the bottom P. It is secured with glue and face nailed flush with the top surface of the shelf. Install 2" wood screws in counterbored holes through the outside edge of the stiles into the middle rail. Fill the holes with wood plugs and sand flush. Cut the top rail T and clamp it in place. Do not secure it at this time because you want to mark the center stile to install dowels in the top and bottom rails.

13 Align the center stile U with equal spacing on both sides and mark the dowel positions. After drilling, insert the dowels and clamp the center stile in place. Glue and face nail the top rail flush with the top surface of the top board. Again, use 2" screws in counterbored holes through the outside edge of the stiles into the top rail. Fill the holes with wood plugs. Fill all the nail holes with colored putty to match your finish. With a ⅜" roundover bit, round over the outside edges of the outer stiles, the lower edge of the middle rail and inside edges of the outside stiles in the lower opening. Be sure to stop rounding over the edges of the outer stiles ¾" from the top so the crown moulding fits tightly to the cabinet. Drill the adjustable shelf pin holes in the same manner as the credenza.

14 Cut the two solid oak shelf back boards V as detailed in the Materials List. Attach each one flush with the back edge of the side boards using glue and 1½" wood screws.

15 Prepare two triangle top boards W, as shown in the illustration. Attach each one flush with the top surface of the upper section using glue and 1½" wood screws. Install the screws through the front edge of the triangle boards; the crown moulding will cover that edge.

16 Cut the six shelves X as shown in the illustration. Use a compass to draw the arc and cut with a jigsaw. Clamp all six shelves together and sand all of them as one unit to ensure they are identical. Sand the shelves, then round over the top and bottom edges of the radius curve with a ⅜" roundover bit. Attach the shelves with glue and screws. Position the shelves to suit your needs, but try and align them with the ⅜"-diameter shelf pin holes. If that position is suitable, screws can be inserted through the shelf pin holes into the shelf boards. If the pin holes don't align with the shelves, use two screws through the back board V into the shelf, and one directly behind the upper stile. Fill the counterbored holes with wood plugs.

Construction Notes

I ordered two ¼"-thick by 10⅛"-deep by 50⅜"-long tempered glass shelves for the upper section of the cabinet. Verify the measurements on your cabinet before ordering the glass.

You'll need four doors 12⅜"-wide by 28½"-high that are designed to accept glass center panels. They are installed with European hidden hinges. For the upper section doors, I used Blum Compact 33 style face frame hinges because of the small stile mounting plate. However, any European-style hinge will work with these doors, and many of the traditional-style hinges will work equally well.

I finished my cabinet with three coats of oil-based polyurethane. I cut the first coat with thinner by 10% and sanded with 220-grit paper between each coat.

The final color, your décor and the type of wood used will determine your finish. However, this cabinet will look great in whatever wood or color you decide to use. Installing lights is optional. I'm a bit of a gadget nut so I installed one 36" fluorescent lamp on top of the cabinet, one behind the hutch top rail and another behind the hutch middle rail.

I found a unique three-lever switch at my local home improvement center that I installed in a single surface-mounted electrical box. I installed the box behind the middle rail where it cannot be seen. I routed the wires behind the back board to an octagon junction box on top of the cabinet. Then I had an electrician connect a supply wire from the service panel to power the lights. While the electrician was there, I had him check my cabinet wiring.

There's not too much involved when installing this cabinet. I suggest you secure the top section to the base with screws through the underside of the credenza top and into the upper cabinet sides. Also, as mentioned previously, the cabinet is tall and shallow so I strongly suggest you attach it to the wall studs with a few 3" screws, just to be safe.

17 Any style of top moulding can be applied. I used 3¼" crown moulding. Some of the angles are tricky, but remember, when cutting angles in crown moulding you should place it upside down in the miter box. The front angle on my cabinet was 41°, but yours may be slightly different. I cut each moulding at 20.5° to equal the 41° corner. There are also two little pieces of moulding that are required on each end, and the angle can be a test of your cutting skills. To make matters more complicated, the moulding is only ¾"-long at the bottom. Take your time and make a couple of test cuts. All that's required is patience to get a nice tight fit.

credenza & bookcase

Here is a project that will go a long way toward meeting our home office storage requirements. This credenza and bookcase hutch project is an ideal place to store all your stationery and reference materials. Everything is stored in one place so it's a breeze to quickly get what you need. The door cabinets and drawer assembly can be modified to meet your specific needs. Or, leave that section out and the credenza can be used as a desk or worktable because it's 30" high.

Once again I've used one of my favorite building materials — multi-core veneer-covered plywood. It's strong, stable, and can be glued, screwed or nailed. Threaded fasteners work great in this material as long as the proper pilot hole is drilled. Plate joinery, commonly called biscuit joints, is another option that I often use with great success when building furniture with this material.

The credenza top and cabinet legs are solid wood. I've opted for red oak once again but any wood species that matches your décor is perfectly acceptable.

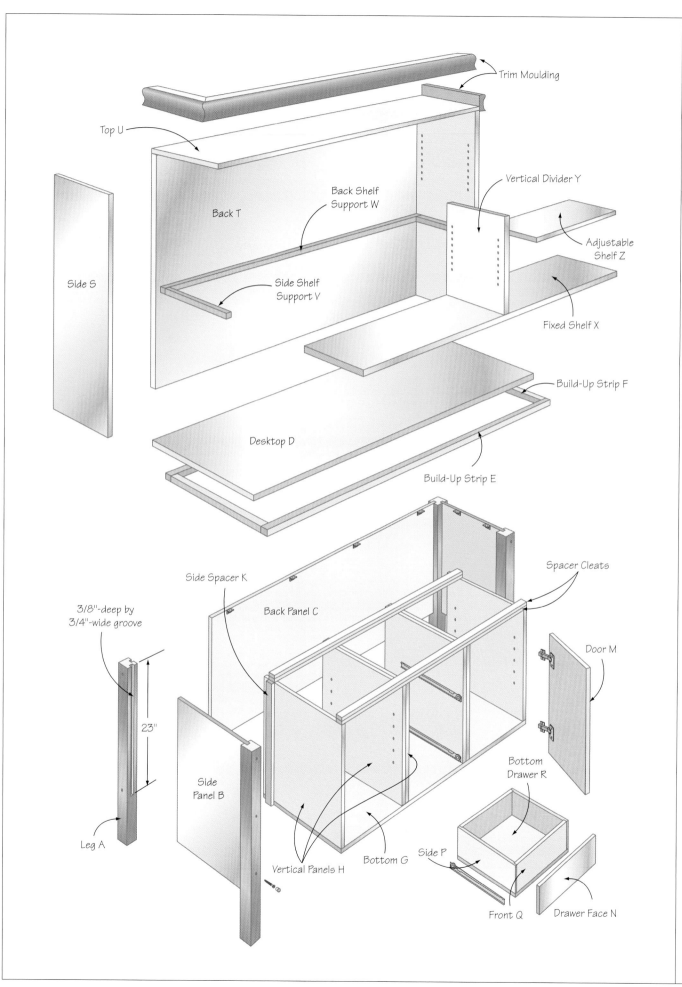

Trim Moulding

Top U

Back Shelf
Support W

Vertical Divider Y

Back T

Adjustable
Shelf Z

Side S

Side Shelf
Support V

Fixed Shelf X

Build-Up Strip F

Desktop D

Build-Up Strip E

Spacer Cleats

Side Spacer K

Back Panel C

3/8"-deep by
3/4"-wide groove

Door M

23"

Bottom
Drawer R

Side
Panel B

Vertical Panels H

Bottom G

Side P

Leg A

Front Q

Drawer Face N

84

HARDWARE AND SUPPLIES

Screws

Nails

Glue

Biscuits or dowels

Three-quarter extension
drawer glides

Full-extension drawer glides
for the file drawer

107° hidden hinges

Drawer and door handles

Metal brackets

Adjustable shelf pins

REFERENCE	QUANTITY	PART	STOCK	THICKNESS	(mm)	WIDTH	(mm)	LENGTH	(mm)
A	4	legs	solid oak	1⁵⁄₈	(41)	1⁵⁄₈	(41)	29¼	(743)
B	2	side panels	oak plywood	¾	(19)	23	(584)	17	(432)
C	1	back	oak plywood	¾	(19)	23	(584)	56	(1422)
D	1	desktop	veneer PB	¾	(19)	21½	(546)	60½	(1537)
E	2	back/front buildup strips	solid wood	¾	(19)	¾	(19)	60½	(1537)
F	2	side buildup strips	solid wood	¾	(19)	¾	(19)	20	(508)
G	1	bottom	oak plywood	¾	(19)	18¼	(464)	55¼	(1403)
H	6	vertical panels	oak plywood	¾	(19)	18¼	(464)	20¾	(527)
J	4	spacer cleats	oak plywood	¾	(19)	1½	(38)	55¼	(1403)
K	2	side spacers	oak plywood	⁷⁄₁₆	(11)	1½	(38)	20¾	(527)
L	2	shelves	oak plywood	¾	(19)	15⁷⁄₈	(403)	18	(457)
M	2	doors	oak plywood	¾	(19)	17	(432)	21⁷⁄₈	(556)
N	2	drawer faces	oak plywood	¾	(19)	10⁷⁄₈	(276)	19¾	(502)
P	4	drawer sides	Birch ply	½	(13)	8⁷⁄₈	(225)	18	(457)
Q	4	drawer front/back	Birch ply	½	(13)	8⁷⁄₈	(225)	17¼	(438)
R	2	drawer bottoms	Birch ply	½	(13)	17¾	(451)	18	(457)

BOOKCASE HUTCH

REFERENCE	QUANTITY	PART	STOCK	THICKNESS	(mm)	WIDTH	(mm)	LENGTH	(mm)
S	2	sides	oak plywood	¾	(19)	11¼	(286)	47¾	(1213)
T	1	back	oak plywood	¾	(19)	47¾	(1213)	60	(1524)
U	1	top	oak plywood	¾	(19)	12	(305)	60	(1524)
V	2	side shelf supports	solid wood	¾	(19)	1½	(38)	11	(279)
W	1	back shelf support	oak plywood	¾	(19)	1½	(38)	58½	(1486)
X	1	fixed bottom shelf	oak plywood	¾	(19)	11¼	(286)	58½	(1486)
Y	1	vertical divider	oak plywood	¾	(19)	11¼	(286)	27¼	(692)
Z	2	adjustable shelves	oak plywood	¾	(19)	11¼	(286)	28¹³⁄₁₆	(729)

1 Prepare the four legs for the storage credenza by cutting them to size. The legs require a groove that's ¾"-wide by ⅜"-deep by 23"-long measured from the top of each leg. Two of the legs need a groove on one face. And the two back legs require two grooves on adjoining faces. Center the grooves on the leg faces. The simplest way to make the grooves is with a ¾"-wide router bit in a table-mounted router.

2 Replace the straight router bit with a ⅜" roundover bit and ease all the edges on each leg. Now is an ideal time to sand the legs.

3 The straight router bit will leave a rounded end on each groove. Use a harp chisel to square the ends so the panels will fit correctly.

4 Cut the two side and back panels to size. The panel ends fit in the grooves of the legs with the double-grooved legs at the back. Put glue in the joint and drive 2" wood screws through the legs and into the panel ends. Two screws per panel end will secure the joint. Drill a pilot hole for the screws and a counterbored ⅜" hole for the screw head. Fill the holes with wood plugs and sand smooth.

5 Attach seven right-angle brackets to the top edge of the panels. Two per side and three on the back panel will be used to secure the credenza top.

6 The finished size for the solid wood top will be 21½"-deep by 60½"-wide. Glue up enough ¾"-thick boards to form a top that's about 1" greater in size (biscuit joints are an ideal way to do this). A jointer will dress the edges perfectly, or you can get acceptable glue edges by cutting the boards on a well-tuned table saw. If you don't have a jointer and your saw can't cut a fine edge, most lumberyards will dress the boards for a small fee.

Tip

Don't clamp the boards too tightly when edge joining. Excessive pressure will squeeze out all the glue and the joint will fail. And you shouldn't have to force the joints together if properly edge-dressed.

7 Sand the top smooth and trim to the correct finished size. Attach the build-up strips and secure with glue and brad nails. This will make the top appear thicker and heavier.

8 | Use a small circular object to draw an arc at each corner of the top. Remove the wood outside the arc with a belt sander to round each corner. Next, install a ⅜" roundover bit in your router and dress the bottom and top edges.

9 | Attach the top to the credenza base with ⅝"-long screws through the right-angle brackets. Verify that the top overhangs all leg faces by 1" before installing the screws. Do not use glue so the top can expand and contract during humidity level changes.

Tip

This panel/leg construction method is solid and the design is very versatile. You can stop at this point if all you require is a great little worktable or shallow desk.

10 | Cut all the panels for the drawer/door compartment. Apply iron-on wood veneer edge tape to the front long edge of the bottom board, the long edge of one spacer cleat, and the long front edge of each vertical panel.

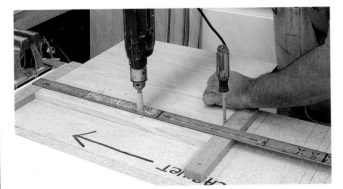

11 | Drill holes in four of the vertical panels for the adjustable shelf pins you plan to use. You can make a simple shelf pin hole jig with flat iron and a couple of pieces of scrap lumber. Drill holes in the iron, spacing them about 1½" apart. Attach the iron to two wood cleats and use a dowel rod mounted on the drill bit to limit the hole depth.

12 | Assemble the credenza with glue and 2" screws according to the illustration. The drawers will be in the center so the four panels with the shelf pin holes will be located facing each other on the two outside compartments. The cleat with the veneered edge is the lower front spacer cleat. Attach the front cleats flush with the front edge of the vertical panels. The rear cleats are spaced 1" in from the ends of all the panels to clear the countertop clips. Verify that the vertical panels are aligned and oriented correctly. The panels must be parallel to each other so the drawer hardware will operate properly.

13 Glue and nail the ⁷⁄₁₆" spacer cleats on the rear outside faces of each end panel, 1" in from the back edge.

14 Lay the credenza on its back and install the compartment. Use 2" screws through the front panels into the front legs. Use 1½" screws through the rear end of each outside panel, through the side spacers, and into the inside face of each end panel. Drive an additional four 2" screws through the outside face of the rear credenza panel into the back edge of the bottom compartment board. Cut and apply edge tape to one front edge of both adjustable shelf boards.

16 Cut all the drawer parts to size. Remember to rabbet the back and front ends of each side ¼" deep by ½" wide. Once again, I've used ½"-thick Baltic birch plywood as I feel it's one of the best choices for office furniture drawer boxes. Follow the assembly procedures in chapter four. The finished size of each drawer is 9⅜"-high by 18¾"-wide by 18"-deep. Install the bottom-mounted drawer glide and test fit both boxes. The first box is mounted ⅛" above the bottom board, and there should be a 1" space between the bottom and top box.

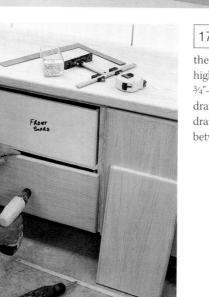

15 The finished size for each door is 17"-wide by 21⅞"-high. You'll need two ¾"-thick wood veneer plywood panels 16"-wide by 20⅞"-high and about 15' of ½"-high by ¾"-thick solid wood to edge the panels. Build the two doors following the same procedures as detailed in chapter six. Round over the front face edges with a ⅜" router bit, drill the hinge holes and install the doors following the steps in chapter five.

17 Two drawer faces, ¾"-thick by 10⅞"-high by 19¾"-wide, are required. They are built to match the door style with a blank ¾" veneer panel that's 9⅞" high by 18¾" wide. The panel is edged with ½"-high by ¾"-thick solid wood. Secure the drawer faces to the drawer boxes using four 1"-long screws from inside the drawer. The height of both drawer faces, plus a ⅛" space between them, should equal the door height.

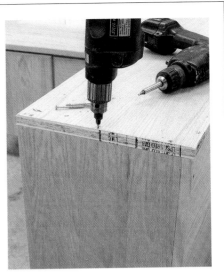

18　The two side and vertical panels for the bookcase hutch require adjustable shelf pin holes. Begin drilling the holes starting 3" from the top edge of each board to a measurement 24" below the top edges. Space the holes 1¼" apart. The side panels each have two rows of holes on the inside face while the vertical divider (Y) requires holes on both faces. Drill the holes all the way through the divider panel. Apply wood edge veneer tape to one long edge on each board.

19　Prepare the backboard by applying wood veneer tape to two short edges. These edges will be visible on each side of the hutch. Attach the side boards to the backboard with glue and 2"-long screws. The outside faces of the side boards should be flush with the ends of the backboard and the shelf pin holes oriented properly.

20　Install the top board on the top edges of the side and back boards using glue and 2" screws. The edges of this panel do not require wood veneer tape, as they will be hidden with trim moulding. It isn't necessary to hide the screw heads, as the top will be on the credenza and over 6' in height.

21　The lower fixed shelf supports are made with 1×2 solid wood. They are cut at 45° to meet in the back corners. Before cutting the miters, round over the bottom edge as well as the front ends on the side supports. Use glue and 1¼" screws to secure the supports. The screws on the outside face of each side panel should be installed in counterbored holes that can be filled with wood plugs. The supports are secured 28" below the underside of the top board.

22　Dress one long front edge of the bottom fixed shelf with wood edge tape. Put the shelf on the supports; secure with glue and brad nails.

23　Apply wood edge tape to the front of the vertical divider and secure it in place. Use glue and 2" screws through the top and bottom boards. The holes on the underside of the bottom board should be counterbored and filled with plugs.

24　Install trim moulding around the top board. I am using the same trim moulding as in chapter six to match the desk hutch. Cut the two adjustable shelves, tape the front edges, and install them on shelf pins.

corner cabinet

A corner china and display cabinet is one of the most popular woodworking projects — if not the most popular. When you talk about cabinets someone is sure to mention their desire for a corner cabinet. If you make one and show it to family and friends, be prepared to make a few more!

I've applied moulding to the top and bottom of this cabinet to match existing furniture. It is a simple, rounded-over trim with very little detail. However, you can dramatically change the looks by installing crown or any of the more intricate mouldings available. The basic design can be transformed into any period-style furniture with the appropriate base and top moulding.

I know that this cabinet project seems to be complicated at first glance, and some woodworkers are intimidated by its apparent complexity, but in reality this corner cabinet is easy to build.

I used ¾"-thick veneer plywood for the carcass construction. It's a strong and stable product, and the perfect choice for this corner cabinet. The only solid wood pieces are the trim and door components.

This cabinet features inset cope-and-stick doors. They are made using a rail-and-stile router bit set, as well as a panel-raising bit. These bits are expensive, but if you plan to make a number of doors they are worth the investment. Remember, take your time making these doors and verify all measurements. They will be installed with only a small gap between the face frame and door, so any error will be obvious.

Jeanne and Jack Chaters of Prescott, Ontario, own the beautiful collection of pottery and specialty dishes displayed here.

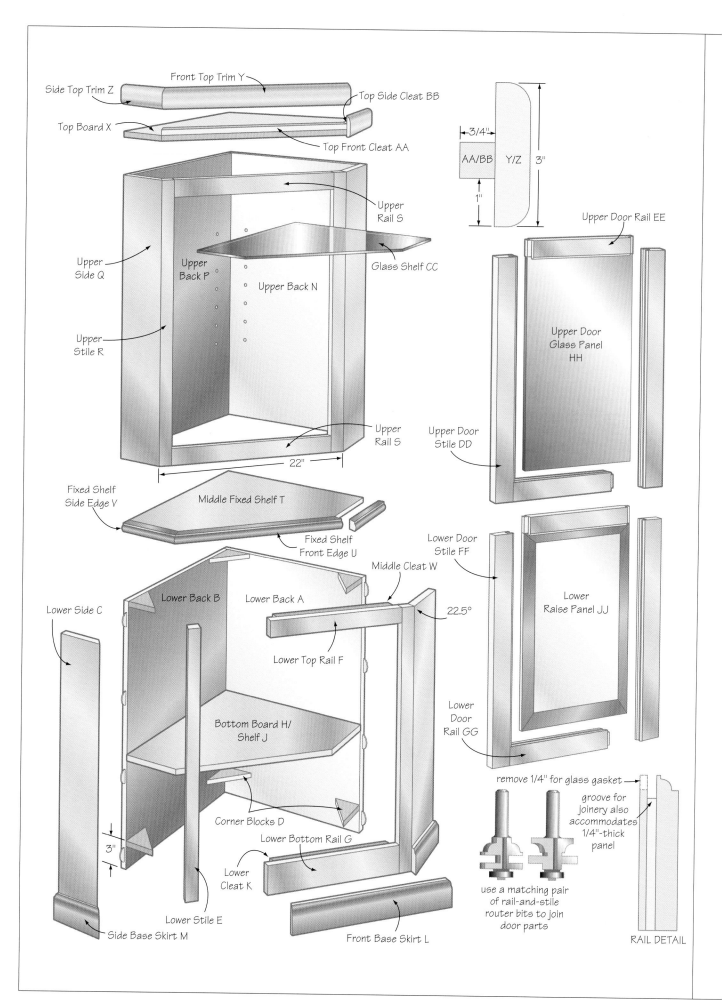

Side Top Trim Z

Front Top Trim Y

Top Side Cleat BB

Top Board X

Top Front Cleat AA

3/4"

AA/BB Y/Z 3"

1"

Upper Door Rail EE

Upper Rail S

Upper Side Q

Upper Back P

Upper Back N

Glass Shelf CC

Upper Door Glass Panel HH

Upper Stile R

Upper Door Stile DD

Upper Rail S

22"

Fixed Shelf Side Edge V

Middle Fixed Shelf T

Fixed Shelf Front Edge U

Middle Cleat W

Lower Door Stile FF

Lower Back B

Lower Back A

22.5°

Lower Side C

Lower Raise Panel JJ

Lower Top Rail F

Bottom Board H/ Shelf J

Lower Door Rail GG

3"

Corner Blocks D

remove 1/4" for glass gasket

groove for joinery also accommodates 1/4"-thick panel

Lower Bottom Rail G

Lower Cleat K

Lower Stile E

use a matching pair of rail-and-stile router bits to join door parts

Side Base Skirt M

Front Base Skirt L

RAIL DETAIL

REFERENCE	QUANTITY	PART	STOCK	THICKNESS	(mm)	WIDTH	(mm)	LENGTH	(mm)	COMMENTS
A	1	lower back	oak plywood	3/4	(19)	22¾	(578)	36	(914)	
B	1	lower back	oak plywood	3/4	(19)	22	(559)	36	(914)	
C	2	lower sides	oak plywood	3/4	(19)	8	(203)	36	(914)	angle cut at 22.5°
D	6	corner blocks	oak	3/4	(19)	3	(76)	3	(76)	right-angle triangle
E	2	lower stiles	oak	3/4	(19)	1½	(38)	36	(914)	angle cut at 22.5°
F	1	lower top rail	oak	3/4	(19)	2	(51)	19	(483)	
G	1	lower bottom rail	oak	3/4	(19)	4	(102)	19	(483)	
H	1	bottom board	oak plywood	3/4	(19)	24	(610)	24	(610)	cut as detailed
J	1	shelf	oak plywood	3/4	(19)	24	(610)	24	(610)	cut as detailed
K	1	lower cleat	oak	3/4	(19)	3/4	(19)	19	(483)	
L	1	front base skirt	oak	3/4	(19)	3	(76)	22⅝	(575)	angle cut
M	2	side base skirts	oak	3/4	(19)	3	(76)	8¼	(21)	angle cut
N	1	upper back	oak plywood	3/4	(19)	22¾	(578)	36	(914)	
P	1	upper back	oak plywood	3/4	(19)	22	(559)	36	(914)	
Q	2	upper sides	oak plywood	3/4	(19)	8	(203)	36	(914)	angle cut at 22.5°
R	2	upper sides	oak	3/4	(19)	1½	(38)	36	(914)	angle cut at 22.5°
S	2	upper rails	oak	3/4	(19)	1½	(38)	19	(483)	
T	1	middle fixed shelf	oak plywood	3/4	(19)	24	(610)	24	(610)	cut as detailed
U	1	fixed shelf front edge	oak	3/4	(19)	1¼	(32)	23¾	(603)	angle cut
V	2	fixed shelf side edges	oak	3/4	(19)	1¼	(32)	8½	(603)	angle cut
W	1	middle cleat	oak	3/4	(19)	3/4	(19)	19	(483)	
X	1	top board	oak plywood	3/4	(19)	24	(610)	24	(610)	
Y	1	front top trim	oak	3/4	(19)	3	(76)	22½	(572)	angle cut
Z	2	side top trim	oak	3/4	(19)	3	(76)	8⅜	(222)	angle cut
AA	1	top front cleat	oak	3/4	(19)	3/4	(19)	22½	(572)	angle cut
BB	2	top side cleats	oak	3/4	(19)	3	(76)	8⅜	(222)	angle cut
CC	2	shelves	glass	1/4	(6)	24	(610)	24	(610)	cut as detailed//use tempered glass
DD	2	upper door stiles	oak	3/4	(19)	2¼	(57)	33	(838)	
EE	2	upper door rails	oak	3/4	(19)	2¼	(57)	15½	(394)	dimensions based on cutter set used
FF	2	lower door stiles	oak	3/4	(19)	2¼	(57)	30	(762)	
GG	2	lower door rails	oak	3/4	(19)	2¼	(57)	15½	(394)	dimensions based on cutter set used
HH	1	upper door	glass	11/16	(18)	15 1/16	(383)	29 1/16	(738)	dimensions based on cutter set used
JJ	1	lower raised panel	oak	5/8-3/4	(16-19)	15¼	(387)	26¼	(667)	see step No. 22 for panel thickness details

Tip

If you are having difficulty achieving a tight joint between the face frame stiles and side boards, increase the stile angle to 23°. This ensures that the stile front edge contacting the angled edge of the side board will be the first point of contact between the two boards. This is a technique often used by trim carpenters to ensure a tight joint where it's most visible.

1 Cut the two lower back panels A and B to size as detailed in the Materials List. Join them with biscuits or 2" screws and glue. Each back should measure 22" on the inside face. Notice that back A is ¾" wider than B to account for the overlap joint.

2 The lower side panels C are ¾"-thick plywood veneer with a 22.5° angle on one long edge. Join them to the back panels with biscuits and glue.

3 The six corner blocks D are installed with glue and screws in pilot holes. The three upper blocks are attached flush with the upper edges of the side and back panels. The lower blocks are secured with their top faces 3" above the bottom edges of the cabinet. These support blocks are right-angle triangles cut from 1×4 stock.

4 Cut the two stiles and two rails E, F and G for the lower face frame using ¾"-thick solid wood. Each stile has a 22.5° outside edge to match the cuts on the side panels. Notice that the bottom rail is 4" high and the top is 2" high. Join the stiles to both rails using glue and screws in counterbored holes, making certain the screw heads are below the surface. Two 2" screws and glue per joint will secure the face frame.

6 Create a template for the base bottom board and shelf, H and J. Trace around the perimeter of the base and carefully cut the template. Trace the pattern on a piece of ¾"-thick veneer plywood and cut ¾" inside all the lines for the bottom fixed board. Use the pattern once again and cut ¹³⁄₁₆" inside the perimeter of the trace lines for the adjustable lower shelf. Attach the lower cleat K to the inside face of the lower rail. It will be aligned so its top surface is 3" above the bottom edge. Set the bottom board on the corner blocks and cleat. Secure this board with 1¼" screws and glue, in piloted holes, through the cleats and corner blocks.

5 Join the face frame to the cabinet carcass using biscuits and glue. Clamp the joint tightly until the glue sets.

Tip

You can easily cut the 45° angles on your table saw by making a cutting sled. It's simply a piece of 1/2" plywood with a 1/2" wood cleat running in the miter gauge tracks. The sled fence is set to 45° and secured in place.

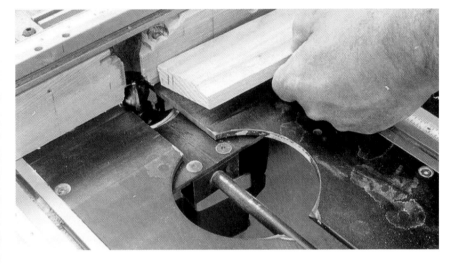

7 My base skirt is 3" high with a decorative edge on the top. For this project I used a cove bit in my router table to complete the cuts. However, any decorative trim bit can be used.

8 Install the base skirt boards L and M using glue and 1½" screws. Drive the screws from the inside to secure the boards.

10 Follow the Materials List and prepare the two stiles R, and two rails S for the upper face frame, which is assembled using the same techniques as the lower frame. Notice that the rails are 1½" high for this frame assembly. Attach the face frame to the upper carcass using biscuits and glue.

9 Cut the upper backs N and P, and the two sides Q. Follow the same procedures when building the upper carcass that were used for the lower case. Use glue and biscuits, dowels or screws when assembling the carcass, making sure the joints are at 90° to each other.

12 Sand the middle board, then round over the upper and lower edges of the hardwood face. Use a ⅜"-radius roundover bit in your router.

11 Trace the middle fixed shelf pattern on a piece of ¾"-thick veneer plywood using the template. This shelf T is cut ⅜" inside the trace lines on the side and front edges, U and V. The back edges are cut on the template lines. Use biscuits to attach a hardwood edge that's 1¼" wide to the sides and front edges. Join the corners with 22.5° angles and clamp until the adhesive is set.

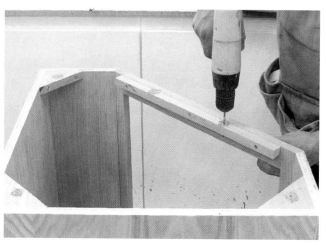

13 Attach the wood cleat W to the back face of the lower face frame top rail. Secure it flush with the rail's top edge. Use glue and 1¼" screws to secure the cleat. Drill through pilot holes in the cleat and three corner blocks for screws to attach the upper section.

14 Secure the middle fixed shelf T to the bottom of the upper section using glue and 2" screws. Align this board with its two back edges flush with the back faces of the upper section back boards.

15 Use the template to trace another pattern on a ¾"-thick veneer plywood panel. This will be the top board X for the upper carcass. The board is cut following the template trace lines. Attach it to the cabinet with all edges flush to the outside faces of the upper carcass. Use glue and 2" screws.

16 Attach the upper cabinet section to the lower cabinet. Use glue and 1¼"-long screws through the cleat W and corner blocks D to secure the sections. Attach the upper and lower carcass making sure their backs are aligned.

17 The top moulding Y and Z has been designed to match existing furniture. However, any style of moulding can be used. I have attached a ¾"-square cleat to the back side of a ¾"-thick by 3"-high hardwood board with rounded edges. Screws have been used in pilot holes to secure the moulding on the cabinet.

18 Cut a shelf hole jig 36" long for the upper section, and 30" long for the lower section. Drill a row of pilot holes in the jig spaced 2" apart. Drill through the center of a wood dowel and leave it on the drill bit to act as a stop to limit the holes' depth. Drill holes in the back and side panels for the shelf pins you plan to use. I used ⁵⁄₁₆"-diameter solid brass pins.

Making the Doors

Trace the middle fixed shelf pattern on a piece of ¾"-thick veneer plywood using the template. This shelf T is cut ⅜" inside the trace lines on the side and front edges, U and V. The back edges  are cut on the template lines. Use biscuits to attach a hardwood edge that's 1¼" wide to the sides and front edges. Join the corners with 22.5° angles and clamp until the adhesive is set.

Sand the middle board, then round over the upper and lower edges of the hardwood face. Use a ⅜"-radius roundover bit in your router.

Secure the middle fixed shelf T to the bottom of the upper section using glue and 2" screws. Align this board with its two back edges flush with the back faces of the upper section back boards.

Attach the wood cleat W to the back face of the lower face frame top rail. Secure it flush with the rail's top edge. Use glue and 1¼" screws to secure the cleat. Drill through pilot holes in the cleat and three corner blocks for screws to attach the upper section.

Use the template to trace another pattern on a ¾"-thick veneer plywood panel. This will be the top board X for the upper carcass. The board is cut following the template trace lines. Attach it to the cabinet with all edges flush to the outside faces of the upper carcass. Use glue and 2" screws.

Attach the upper cabinet section to the lower cabinet. Use glue and 1¼"-long screws through the cleat W and corner blocks D to secure the sections. Attach the upper and lower carcass making sure their backs are aligned.

I have used a rubber gasket designed specifically for securing glass panels in cope-and-stick doors. However, there are many ways to install the glass, including clips and silicone adhesive.

There are also dozens of hinge options for the doors. Your choice depends on the style of cabinet, other furnishings in the room and personal taste. I used a traditional hinge that doesn't require a mortise because it folds into itself. It is also ¹⁄₁₆" thick, which is the spacing I require around my inset door. There should be a ¹⁄₁₆" gap around the perimeter of each door. Trial fit the doors and plane or sand them to achieve the perfect fit.

Select your handles, latch and lamp assembly. I used a plain knob to match the hinge finish, and a small magnetic catch. The lamp is a quartz halogen fixture with a built-in switch.

Construction Notes

Complete the cabinet by sanding all the surfaces and applying a finish. My cabinet has a custom stain and three coats of polyurethane. For increased protection and a smooth finish, I applied a coat of hard clear paste wax with No. 0000 steel wool.

As I previously mentioned, this corner cabinet is trimmed in a contemporary style. But you can change the cabinet style to traditional, classic or any other by simply installing a different top and base moulding. The basic case construction is the same no matter which style you choose. This cabinet size suits my requirements.

The dimensions in the Materials List are only a guide. Alter the height, back board width or opening to suit your needs. The design calls for ¾"-thick plywood veneer for the case construction. It's an expensive sheet material, but one that's strong and well worth using for this project. The use of this material eliminates the need for added structural support frames, so in this case it is cost effective.

You might consider another design change: The upper section side boards may be replaced with a wooden frame to support a glass panel. It's dramatically different and increases the view inside the upper display area. If you have a collection that requires maximum exposure, glass side panels might be the solution.

contemporary display and storage cabinet

Contemporary furniture is most often flat paneled without the detailed mouldings common to more traditional cabinets. Adding accent strips or color differences creates visual interest. I decided to add two bands of dark walnut as a sharp contrast to the natural finished oak. The hardware also has clean, simple lines, which are a common design treatment of modern-styled furniture.

Three glass shelves provide a surprising amount of display space. These shelves are 12½" deep, so there's room for large collectibles.

The greater depth also increases the cabinet's stability. However, the depth is a design choice and can be altered to suit your collection. Build it at least 12" deep if you want a freestanding unit, and less than 12" if you plan on anchoring the cabinet to a wall. With all its glass, it would be very dangerous to have this cabinet topple. If you have any concern about its stability, please anchor the cabinet to a wall stud.

The impressive collection of antique photographic equipment shown here is a dramatic contrast to the modern styling of this cabinet and makes for a visual treat.

Michael Bowie of Lux Photography in Ottawa, Ontario, owns the camera collection. Michael is responsible for the lead project photos, and is also the technical expert for the step-by-step photography in all of my books.

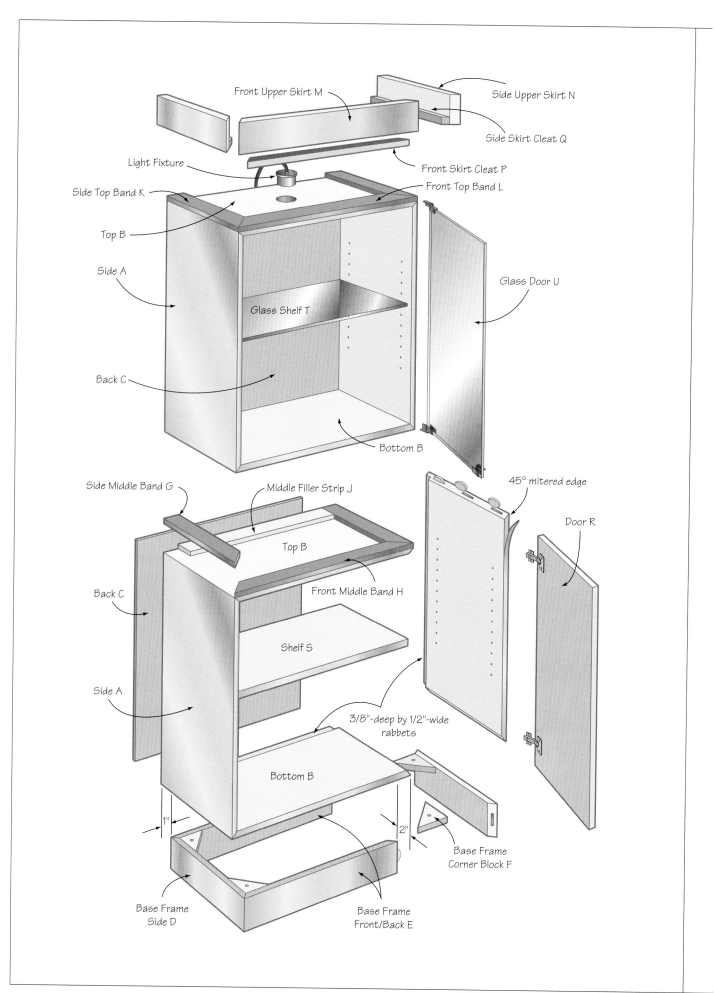

Front Upper Skirt M

Side Upper Skirt N

Side Skirt Cleat Q

Light Fixture

Front Skirt Cleat P

Side Top Band K

Front Top Band L

Top B

Side A

Glass Door U

Glass Shelf T

Back C

Bottom B

Side Middle Band G

Middle Filler Strip J

45° mitered edge

Door R

Top B

Back C

Front Middle Band H

Shelf S

Side A

3/8"-deep by 1/2"-wide rabbets

Bottom B

1"

2"

Base Frame Corner Block F

Base Frame Side D

Base Frame Front/Back E

REFERENCE	QUANTITY	PART	STOCK	THICKNESS	(mm)	WIDTH	(mm)	LENGTH	(mm)	COMMENTS
A	4	sides	oak PB	3/4	(19)	14	(356)	35	(889)	45° bevel on ends
B	4	tops & bottoms	oak PB	3/4	(19)	14	(356)	42	(1067)	45° bevel on ends
C	2	backs	oak PB	3/4	(19)	34½	(876)	41½	(105)	
D	2	base frame sides	oak PB	½	(13)	3	(76)	12	(305)	45° bevel on ends
E	2	base frame fronts & backs	oak PB	½	(13)	3	(76)	38	(965)	45° bevel on ends
F	4	base frame corner blocks	oak PB	3/4	(19)	3	(76)	3	(76)	cut as right-angle triangle
G	2	side middle bands	oak PB	3/4	(19)	1½	(38)	14	(356)	45° miter one end
H	1	front middle band	oak PB	11/16	(18)	1½	(38)	42	(1067)	45° miter on both ends
J	1	middle filler strip	oak PB	11/16	(18)	2½	(64)	39	(991)	
K	1	side top bands	oak PB	11/16	(18)	1½	(38)	14	(356)	45° miter one end
L	1	front top band	oak PB	3/4	(19)	1½	(38)	42	(1067)	45° miter on both ends
M	1	front upper skirt	oak PB	3/4	(19)	3¼	(83)	42	(1067)	45° miter on both ends
N	2	side upper skirts	oak PB	3/4	(19)	3¼	(83)	14	(356)	45° miter one end
P	1	front skirt cleat	oak PB	3/4	(19)	3/4	(19)	42	(1067)	45° miter on both ends
Q	2	side skirt cleats	oak PB	3/4	(19)	3/4	(19)	14	(356)	45° miter one end
R	2	doors	oak PB	3/4	(19)	34¾	(883)	20¾	(527)	all edges banded with veneer
S	2	lower shelves	oak PB	3/4	(19)	13	(330)	40⅜	(1026)	
T	3	shelves	glass	3/4	(19)	12½	(318)	40½	(470)	tempered
U	2	doors	glass	3/4	(19)	33	(838)	20³⁄₁₆	(513)	

HARDWARE AND SUPPLIES

4 European hinges

4 hinges for glass doors

12 shelf pins for glass shelves

2 door handles

2 magnetic door catches

2 magnetic catches for glass doors

1 flush-mount light

Construction Notes

Before you begin cutting the sides, tops and bottoms to length, consider this option if you don't want the mitered corners. This alternative case construction method using butt joinery is easier than the mitered-corner system.

The butt joinery system uses biscuits or screws and glue. The tops and bottoms sit on the side boards and the exposed edges are covered with heat-activated pre-glued veneer tape. Many woodworkers find this alternative method easier and just as strong. The only change between this and the corner miter joint is the back board rabbet. It must be stopped ¼" short of the ends on the top and bottom boards. Either method is acceptable — the choice is yours. I will detail the corner-miter method in the step-by-step photos in this

chapter. The dimensions given in the Materials List are based on the mitered corner, so change them accordingly if you prefer the butt-joinery system.

1 Rip four lengths of ¾"-thick veneer plywood from two sheets. Each panel will be 14" wide and 96" long. These four panels will be used for the sides, tops and bottom boards, A and B. The panels will be cut to length with 45° miters on both ends. However, one front edge of each panel must have veneer edge tape applied before cutting the miters on a table saw. This will give you well defined angle cuts on the edge tape. Use ⅞"-wide, preglued, heat-activated veneer edge tape that's applied with an iron. Remove the excess wood tape with a trim bit in your router.

2 Miter cut the eight panels — four sides, two tops and two bottoms, at 45° — to the sizes detailed in the Materials List. The sizes stated are at the longest point of the miter cut. The cutting is easily accomplished on a table saw.

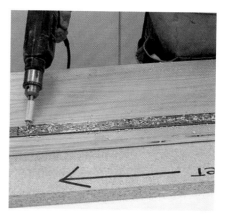

3 Build a simple jig, such as the one shown, to drill two columns of holes in each side panel. These will be used for the adjustable shelf pins and should be the proper diameter for the pins you plan to use. These holes are 3⁄16"-diameter for the brass pins I've chosen. Two mirror-image sets of holes are drilled on the inside face of each panel.

4 Each side, top and bottom panel requires a ⅜"-deep by ½"-wide rabbet to receive the back panel. All cuts are located on the rear inside faces of the panels. Make the rabbet cuts with a table saw, router or router table and straight bit.

5 Use No. 0 biscuits and glue to join the four mitered corners on the upper and lower case. Cut the biscuit slots, being careful not to puncture the outside face of the panel. Clamp each carcass until the adhesive sets.

6 Install the backs C on each carcass, in the rabbets, securing them with glue and nails. Verify the exact measurements before cutting these back boards. Remember, if the back boards are cut square, the cabinet carcass will be square.

7 The base frame is made with ¾"-thick veneer plywood. Miter the ends of the four boards D and E at 45°. Reinforce the corner joints with biscuits and apply glue before clamping the frame. Install the four angled corner blocks F with glue and nails. They will strengthen the base frame, square the corners and will be used to attach the frame to the lower carcass.

8 Attach the base frame to the lower cabinet carcass by drilling a hole through each corner block. Use glue and one 1¼"-long screw through each block into the underside of the cabinet carcass. Align the frame so it's 2" back from the front edge and 1" in on each side of the cabinet.

9   The middle banding, G and H, is a darker wood than the cabinet carcass in order to create visual interest. I used walnut to contrast with the lighter oak of the cases. The front band requires a 45° miter on each end. Both sides are cut with the same miter on the front end only. The filler strip J is a piece of any ¾"-thick material in your shop and is installed to support the back edge of the upper carcass. Attach all the strips flush with the outside faces of the carcass using glue and 1¼"-long screws.

10   Drill a series of ¼"-diameter holes, spaced 6" apart, around the perimeter of the banding and filler strip boards. The holes are drilled through the banding and lower carcass top board. They will be used as locator holes when joining the upper with the lower carcass.

11   Apply glue on the banding and filler strip boards. Install the top section flush with the banding face edges. Use 2"-long screws in the previously drilled pilot holes to secure the sections.

12   Lay the cabinet on its back. Cut and install the top banding K and L following the same procedures as the lower banding. Use glue and 1¼"-long screws to attach the three boards.

13 The upper skirt is mainly decorative but serves as a guard to hide the cabinet lamp. The front and side skirts M and N are installed flush with the banding face edges. The corners of the skirt boards are mitered at 45° and ¾"-square cleats P and Q are attached to the skirt boards. These cleats will be used to secure the skirt assembly. Rough cut the three skirt boards a little longer than required, and attach the cleats flush with the lower edges on the back face. Now, miter cut the skirt boards to the lengths given in the Materials List. This procedure will miter both skirt and cleat boards in one operation.

14 Drive 2"-long screws through pilot holes in the cleats to secure the skirt flush with the top banding boards. Use glue on all the joints, including the skirt board corners. Reinforce the skirt corners with a right-angle metal bracket and ⅝"-long screws.

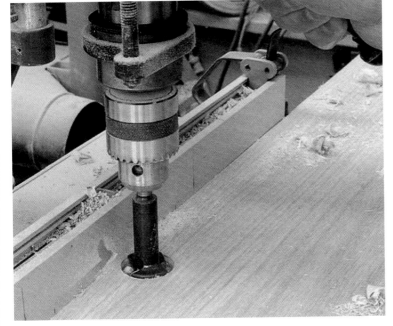

15 Two styles of lower doors R can be installed using full-overlay hidden hinges. The first is an inset door set flush with the cabinet edges, and the second is a full-overlay door that covers the cabinet's front edges. I will be using full-overlay doors but either style is suitable. If you decide to use the inset door style, be sure the cabinet is square. Inset doors reveal a ¹⁄₁₆" gap around the edge, and you will need two doors at 33⅜"-high by 20⅛"-wide. The overlay door width, using full-overlay hidden hinges, is determined by adding 1" to the inside cabinet dimension and dividing by two. For this project, the interior width is 40½"; add 1" and the total is 41½". Dividing that dimension by two means that we need two 20¾" doors for this cabinet. Cut the doors to size, apply heat activated iron-on veneer edge tape to the four edges of each door and drill two 35mm holes per door. The holes are ⅛" from the edge. Space the hinge holes 4" from the top and bottom of each door.

16 To mount the doors, install the 107° hinges with their mounting plates on each door. Hold the door in its open position with a ⅛"-thick spacer between the door edge and cabinet front edge. In this case I've aligned the bottom of the doors flush with the lower edge of the cabinet's bottom board. Drive ⅝"-long screws through the hinge plate holes into the cabinet side board to secure the door. Follow the same procedure for the second door and align if necessary.

17 Cut the two lower shelves S, apply edge tape to the front edge and test fit.

18 Install the tempered glass shelves T. I will be using three shelves that are ¼"-thick with polished edges. My shelf pins are ³⁄₁₆"-diameter solid brass.

19 After verifying your measurements, it is an ideal time to order the tempered glass shelves and door, T and U. It's also the perfect time to apply a finish to the cabinet before installing any hardware. I've used three coats of semigloss polyurethane and sanded with 320-grit sandpaper between each coat. The final finish treatment is a coat of clear paste, applied with No. 0000 steel wool for added protection.

Glass Doors Made Simple

The glass door hinges used here are a simple swing model on a pivot pin, commonly found in hardware or glass supply stores. The hinges are mounted as an inset style and the glass doesn't require any drilled holes. Mount the hinge hardware before ordering the glass, thereby allowing yourself to verify the measurements. Dimensions differ slightly from one hardware manufacturer to the next, so it pays to double-check the dimensions.

20 My lamp assembly is black to match the hinge hardware. Installing the light is optional, but if you do decide to put lights in your cabinet, purchase the unit and follow the manufacturer's instructions.

21 My glass door hinges and lamp assembly are black so I decided to install black door handles. The lower door handles are plain in keeping with the contemporary style of this cabinet. The glass door handles are a metal slip-on type, readily available at hardware stores. The doors are held closed with a magnetic catch.

Construction Notes

The tempered glass shelves are strong and able to support most collectibles. However, if the items are heavy it would be wise to drill a row of support holes for pins in the cabinet back board.

If the items you plan to display are extremely heavy, a wood back or brace can be installed on the rear edge of each shelf. Cut a groove in one edge of a 1×2 board, about ¼" deep, and slip it over the glass shelf. Use adhesive silicon to secure this strong back.

Any dimension of this cabinet can be altered to suit your requirements, and different wood accent strips can be used to match the existing furniture in the room where this cabinet will be used.

If you are comfortable with wood inlay techniques, interesting designs can be used on the lower wood doors. Design possibilities are endless and limited only by your imagination.

tall bookcase

Almost everyone I know could use another bookcase in his or her home. This project can be styled to fit any room, and would be a welcome addition as a storage or showcase cabinet for many items, including books. If you know a child who's an avid collector of things like dolls or racing cars, this is the perfect solution.

This bookcase is built using hidden pocket hole joinery. It's an extremely sturdy unit, which can support the weight of any normal collection. If you need to display unusually heavy items, I'll detail a support option that will increase the load capacity of the shelves.

The most important feature of this bookcase is the adjustable shelf system. You can build a fixed shelf version, but I think you'll find it limiting because all books aren't the same size. Adjustable shelves make this case suitable for any display items.

The project is made with veneer particleboard (PB) and readily available trim and solid wood. You don't need a fully equipped workshop to build this bookcase. A table saw, electric drills and a pocket hole jig are all the tools you'll need.

Once again, I'll follow my process of teaching the building techniques needed to build this project. The object isn't really to build this bookcase to the exact size shown; it's more about using the techniques to build one that meets your needs. The sizes stated are secondary to the process used to build the project.

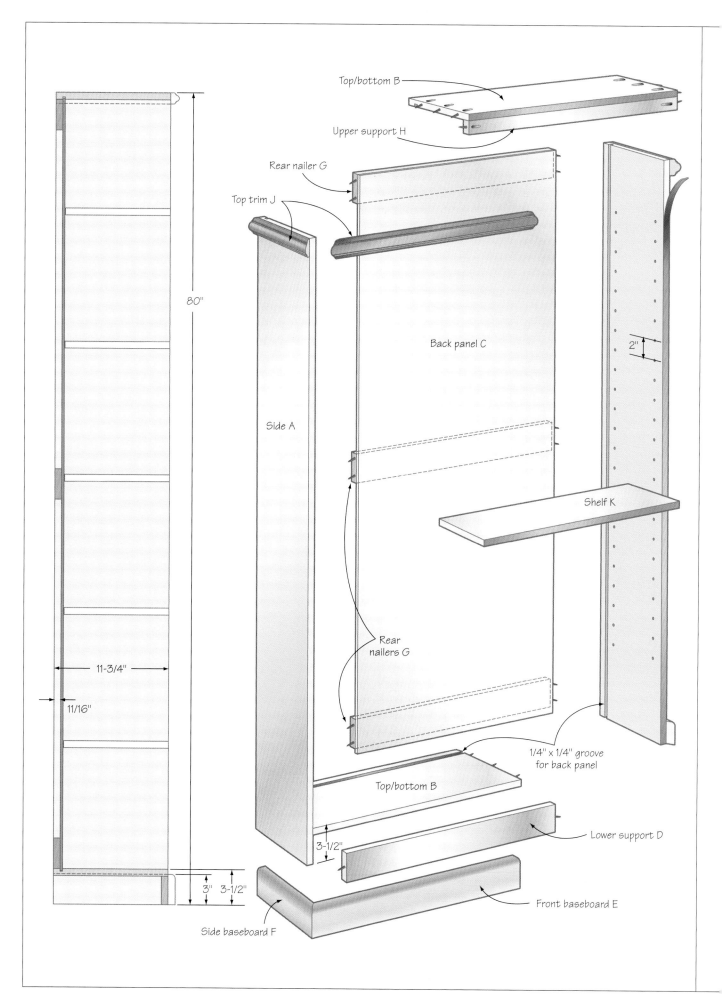

Top/bottom B

Upper support H

Rear nailer G

Top trim J

Side A

Back panel C

2"

80"

Shelf K

Rear
nailers G

11-3/4"

11/16"

1/4" x 1/4" groove
for back panel

Top/bottom B

3-1/2"

Lower support D

3" 3-1/2"

Front baseboard E

Side baseboard F

REFERENCE	QUANTITY	PART	STOCK	THICKNESS	(mm)	WIDTH	(mm)	LENGTH	(mm)
A	2	sides	veneer PB	$^{11}/_{16}$	(18)	$11^{3}/_{4}$	(298)	80	(2032)
B	2	top and bottom	veneer PB	$^{11}/_{16}$	(18)	$11^{3}/_{4}$	(298)	$28^{5}/_{8}$	(727)
C	1	back panel	veneer ply	$^{1}/_{4}$	(6)	$29^{1}/_{8}$	(740)	$76^{1}/_{8}$	(1933)
D	1	lower support	veneer PB	$^{11}/_{16}$	(18)	$2^{13}/_{16}$	(72)	$28^{5}/_{8}$	(727)
E	1	front baseboard	hardwood	$^{3}/_{4}$	(19)	3	(76)	$31^{1}/_{2}$	(800)
F	2	side baseboards	hardwood	$^{3}/_{4}$	(19)	3	(76)	$12^{1}/_{2}$	(318)
G	3	rear nailers	veneer PB	$^{11}/_{16}$	(18)	3	(76)	$28^{5}/_{8}$	(727)
H	1	upper support	veneer PB	$^{11}/_{16}$	(18)	$^{15}/_{16}$	(24)	$28^{5}/_{8}$	(727)
J		top trim	hardwood					60	(1524)
K	5	shelves	veneer PB	$^{11}/_{16}$	(18)	$10^{3}/_{4}$	(273)	$28^{9}/_{16}$	(725)

Note: PB = particleboard.

HARDWARE AND SUPPLIES

Pocket hole screws:
$1^{1}/_{4}$" (32mm)

Wood screws: $1^{1}/_{4}$" (32mm)

Finishing nails

Glue

Shelf pins

Wood veneer edge tape

Wood putty

1 Cut the two sides A as well as the bottom and top B to the sizes indicated in the materials list. Form a ¼"-wide by ¼"-deep groove on the back, inside face of each panel. The back edge of each groove is $^{11}/_{16}$" away from the back edge of sides A to provide space for the rear nailers. Grooves can be cut on a table saw, but you will have to make two passes on each panel to achieve the required width. These grooves can also be cut with a ¼" straight router bit in a handheld or table-mounted router. Test fit a piece of the ¼" back panel to ensure the proper fit in all the grooves.

2 Adjustable shelf pin holes can be easily and accurately drilled using a shop-made jig. Cut a piece of sheet scrap that's 4" wide by 84" long. Attach to the top end a second piece of the same material that's 4" wide by 16" long, forming a T. Be sure to align the pieces at 90°. Drill a column of holes in the center of the jig, about 2" apart, that begins and ends 12" from the bottom and top. The column of holes should be drilled as accurately as possible. The drill bit diameter should suit the adjustable shelf pins you plan to use.

3 Mark the top of each side panel. The top of your jig is always placed at the top edge of the sides. Align the outside edge of the jig to the outside edge of the panel before drilling the column of holes. You'll need two columns on each side panel. Drill through the center of a dowel rod and place it on the bit, butted tight to the drill chuck to expose the length of drill bit needed for the required hole depth. You'll get properly placed holes at the correct depth using this jig method.

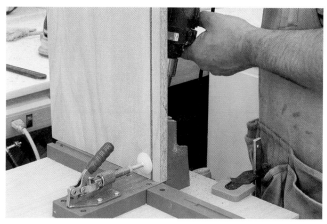

4 Apply matching edge tape to the front edges of the two sides A, top B and bottom B. I'm using oak veneer PB, so I will use pre-glued, iron-on wood-edge veneer tape. Note: Trimming wood veneer can be tricky because some of the wider grain woods, like oak, tend to tear along the grain pattern when using a knife or chisel. I use a flush-trim router bit to dress my wood edge. If you don't have a router, carefully use a sharp hand edge trimmer and sand the edges to make a clean edge.

5 Drill three pocket holes on the ends of each top and bottom B. Both panels will have six pocket holes on the face opposite the groove.

6 Attach the top to the two sides; do not install the bottom at this time. Use 1¼"-long pocket hole screws and wood glue. The top face of this panel is aligned flush with the top edges of the side boards.

7 Cut the back panel C to the size shown in the materials list. Slip it into the side and top board grooves, using a small amount of glue to prevent back panel movement.

8 Install the bottom B using 1¼" pocket hole screws and glue. The back panel C will fit into the groove on the bottom board. Its top face is 3½" above the bottom edges of the side boards.

9 Cut and attach the lower support D. It's used to secure the bottom trim and strengthen the base of the bookcase. Use glue and 1¼" pocket hole screws to install this board. Its front face is aligned flush with the front edges of the side and bottom boards.

10 The base trim boards E and F are ¾"-thick hardwood, and installed flush with the bottom of sides A and lower support board D. Trim boards are installed with glue and 1¼"-long wood screws from the inside. The corners are joined with 45° miters. I am using a simple roundover technique on the top outside edges of my trim boards. However, any style of trim detailing can be done to match existing room furniture.

11 The three rear nailers G will support the back panel and allow you to anchor the cabinet to a wall if necessary. Attach them with pocket hole screws and glue, one at the top, bottom and center of the backboard.

12 The top trim J is a design element only, and can be omitted or changed to a style that suits your needs. I am using a bullnose-style trim that's available at most lumberyards. I will also install the support board H behind the upper trim. It's the same height as the trim, minus the thickness of the top board. Install this support board with glue and pocket hole screws in the front face, as it will be covered by the trim detail. If you are using particleboard or plywood for this support board, apply wood veneer tape to the bottom visible edge.

13 Attach the trim with glue and finishing nails, mitering the corners at 45°. You'll need about 5' of trim to cover the front and two sides.

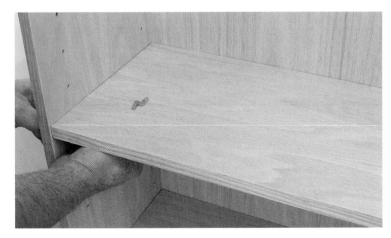

14 If you require only four shelves, this project can be built with one sheet of $^{11}/_{16}$"- or ¾"-thick material and two-thirds of a sheet of ¼" plywood veneer. If you need five shelves like I do, you'll have to buy a part sheet. Apply veneer tape to the front edges and install the shelves on pins. This bookcase was finished with three coats of satin polyurethane.

basic workstation

This simple workstation consists of a file/storage drawer module tower, laminate desktop, bookcase end and a simple hutch. It's built using decorative joinery screws that allow for disassembly. You could use standard biscuit or screw-and-glue joinery, but if you have, say, a college student who is always moving, joinery screws are the answer.

Since computers now play such a large role in our work and school activities, I've included a raised, closed stand attached to the back of the bookcase for the storage of a computer CPU. The desktop is designed so the computer monitor can be placed on the right side. The desk area in front of the chair can be used for paperwork.

A commercially available pull-out keyboard tray also can be attached underneath the desktop, directly in front of the seat space.

The file/storage tower has three utility drawers and a large capacity cabinet for paper storage. The tower top is an ideal place for a printer — it's out of the way but still easily accessible.

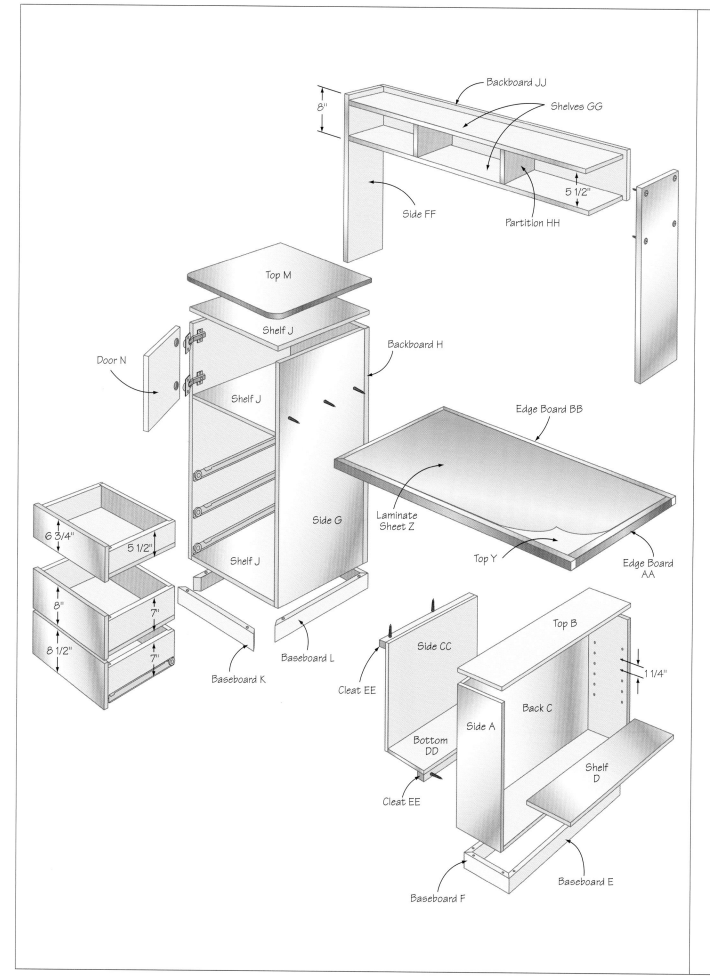

Backboard JJ

Shelves GG

8"

Side FF

5 1/2"

Partition HH

Top M

Shelf J

Door N

Shelf J

Backboard H

Edge Board BB

Shelf J

Side G

Laminate
Sheet Z

Top Y

Edge Board
AA

6 3/4"

5 1/2"

8"

7"

8 1/2"

7"

Baseboard K

Baseboard L

Side CC

Top B

1 1/4"

Cleat EE

Back C

Side A

Bottom
DD

Shelf
D

Cleat EE

Baseboard F

Baseboard E

118

REFERENCE	QUANTITY	PART	STOCK	THICKNESS	(mm)	WIDTH	(mm)	LENGTH	(mm)
A	2	sides	veneer PB	$^{11}/_{16}$	(18)	10	(254)	$27^3/_4$	(705)
B	2	bottom & top	veneer PB	$^{11}/_{16}$	(18)	10	(254)	$23^1/_2$	(597)
C	1	back	veneer PB	$^{11}/_{16}$	(18)	$23^1/_2$	(597)	$26^3/_8$	(670)
D	2	shelves	veneer PB	$^{11}/_{16}$	(18)	$9^1/_4$	(235)	$23^7/_{16}$	(595)
E	2	baseboards	solid wood	$^3/_4$	(19)	$1^1/_2$	(38)	23	(584)
F	2	baseboards	solid wood	$^3/_4$	(19)	$1^1/_2$	(38)	8	(203)
PRINTER TOWER									
G	2	side panels	veneer PB	$^{11}/_{16}$	(18)	$21^3/_4$	(552)	$36^1/_2$	(927)
H	1	back	veneer PB	$^{11}/_{16}$	(18)	18	(457)	$36^1/_2$	(927)
J	3	fixed shelves	veneer PB	$^{11}/_{16}$	(18)	$16^5/_8$	(422)	$21^3/_4$	(552)
K	2	baseboards	solid wood	$^3/_4$	(19)	$1^1/_2$	(38)	16	(406)
L	2	baseboards	solid wood	$^3/_4$	(19)	$1^1/_2$	(38)	$20^1/_2$	(521)
M	1	top	veneer PB	$^{11}/_{16}$	(18)	18	(457)	$23^1/_2$	(570)
N	1	door	veneer PB	$^{11}/_{16}$	(18)	$12^1/_4$	(311)	$17^5/_8$	(448)
DRAWER & DRAWER FRONTS									
P	4	sides	Birch ply	$^1/_2$	(13)	$6^1/_2$	(165)	18	(457)
Q	4	front & back	Birch ply	$^1/_2$	(13)	$6^1/_2$	(165)	$36^1/_2$	(927)
R	2	bottoms	Birch ply	$^1/_2$	(13)	$15^5/_8$	(397)	18	(457)
S	2	sides	Birch ply	$^1/_2$	(13)	5	(127)	18	(457)
T	2	front & back	Birch ply	$^1/_2$	(13)	5	(127)	$15^5/_8$	(397)
U	1	bottom	Birch ply	$^1/_2$	(13)	$15^5/_8$	(397)	18	(457)
V	1	bottom drawer front	veneer PB	$^{11}/_{16}$	(18)	$8^1/_2$	(216)	$17^5/_8$	(448)
W	1	middle drawer front	veneer PB	$^{11}/_{16}$	(18)	8	(203)	$17^5/_8$	(448)
X	1	top drawer front	veneer PB	$^{11}/_{16}$	(18)	$6^3/_4$	(171)	$17^5/_8$	(448)
DESKTOP									
Y	1	top	veneer PB	$^3/_4$	(19)	25	(635)	50	(1270)
Z	1	laminate sheet		N/A		27	(686)	52	(1320)
AA	2	edge boards	solid wood	$^3/_4$	(19)	$1^1/_2$	(38)	25	(635)
BB	2	edge boards	solid wood	$^3/_4$	(19)	$1^1/_2$	(38)	$51^1/_2$	(1308)
CPU COMPARTMENT									
CC	1	side	veneer PB	$^{11}/_{16}$	(18)	19	(483)	19	(483)
DD	1	bottom	veneer PB	$^{11}/_{16}$	(18)	10	(254)	19	(483)
EE	2	cleats	solid wood	$^3/_4$	(19)	$1^1/_2$	(38)	18	(457)
HUTCH									
FF	2	sides	veneer PB	$^{11}/_{16}$	(18)	7	(178)	$29^1/_2$	(749)
GG	2	horizontal shelf	veneer PB	$^{11}/_{16}$	(18)	7	(178)	$47^5/_8$	(1210)
HH	2	vertical partition	veneer PB	$^{11}/_{16}$	(18)	$5^1/_2$	(140)	7	(178)
JJ	1	back	veneer PB	$^{11}/_{16}$	(18)	8	(203)	49	(1245)

HARDWARE AND SUPPLIES

veneer edge
tape

screws

nails

glue

biscuits or dowels

three-quarter extension
drawer glides

full-extension drawer glides
for file drawer

107° hidden hinges

high-pressure laminate

contact cement

cable hole grommets

commercial CD racks (optional)

pull-out keyboard tray

drawer handles

1 Cut the two sides (A), and the top and bottom boards (B). Apply iron-on wood veneer edge tape to one long side on each of the four boards.

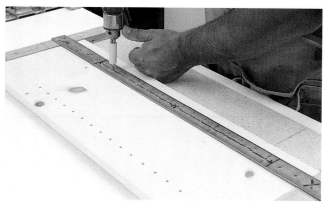

2 Drill holes on the inside face of each side panel for the adjustable shelf pins. You can make a simple jig such as the one shown in the photograph or mark the holes and use a drill press. I spaced my holes 1¼" apart but any spacing is acceptable.

3 The sides are joined to the top and bottom boards. The joint can be made using glue in combination with biscuits, dowels or screws. I have decided to use only decorative assembly screws for easy dismantling and transportation. This type of hardware comes in many forms, such as the big cap screws I'm using, as well as screws with washers. Be sure the hardware you use is designed for PB joinery if that's the material you plan to use. And, always drill the proper size pilot hole for that fastener to achieve maximum hold.

4 Install the inset back with two screws on each edge. Its back face should be set flush with the back edge of the top, bottom and side boards.

Tip

Wood veneer edge tape comes in a number of widths and lengths. The simplest type to apply is the pre-glued material that is heat activated with an iron.

I'm using pine veneer, which trims cleanly with a double-edged trimmer. However, wide-grained woods such as oak should be trimmed with a flush-trim bit in a router.

5 Join the four baseboards with 45° angled cuts at each corner. Use glue and nails to secure the four joints. The outside dimension of the base frame should be 8" deep by 23" long. Attach the frame to the bottom board of the bookcase with 1½"-long screws in counterbored holes. The base frame is attached so it's equally spaced on all four sides.

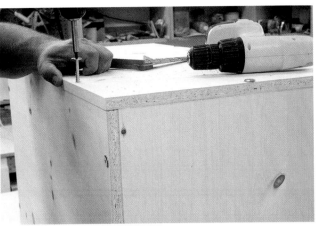

6 Cut the two adjustable shelf boards (D). Apply wood veneer to one long edge on each board. Then prepare the two side panels (G) and the three fixed shelves (J) by applying wood veneer edge tape to one long edge on each side board and one short edge on each of the fixed shelves. The top fixed shelf is installed flush with the top end of the side boards as shown here, and the bottom fixed shelf with the bottom ends. The middle fixed shelf is attached so its top surface is 24" from the bottom ends of each side panel.

7 Apply wood veneer tape to both long edges of the backboard. Secure the backboard to the cabinet so its edges are flush with the top, bottom and both side boards.

8 Join the four baseboards with 45° angled cuts at each corner. Use glue and nails to secure the four joints. The outside dimension of the base frame should be 16" wide by 20½" deep. Attach the frame to the bottom board of the printer tower with 1½"-long screws in counterbored holes. The base frame is attached so it's equally spaced on all four sides.

9 The printer tower top is made from ¹¹⁄₁₆"-thick veneer PB and wood veneer edge tape. Slightly round the front corners of the top with a belt sander. Apply the wood veneer tape with a hot iron. The heat will soften the veneer tape, allowing it to be formed around each front corner, creating a seamless band on the front and two side edges. Then align the top flush with the cabinet back and both side boards. It will overhang in front by ¹¹⁄₁₆". Use four 1¼"-long screws to secure the top from inside the cabinet.

10 Cut all the drawer parts to size following the dimensions given in the cutting list. Refer to chapter three for drawer-building procedures.

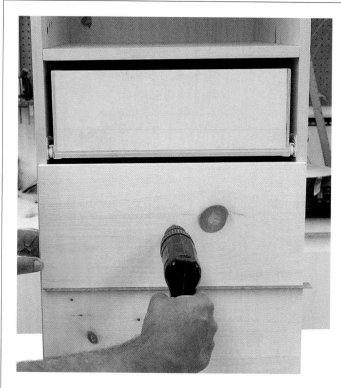

11 Cut the three drawer faces to size as shown in the cutting list. Apply wood veneer edge tape to all the face edges. Install the three drawer faces with a ¹⁄₁₆" space between each. The bottom face is flush with the underside of the bottom fixed shelf. Refer to chapter three for installation tips.

How to Calculate Door Sizes

You can easily calculate the exact width of the door or doors you'll need when using full-overlay hidden hinges. Add 1" to the inside width of the cabinet. That will be your required door size. If you need two doors, simply divide that number by two. For example, a 24"-wide frameless-style cabinet, built with ⅝"-thick sheet goods, has an inside dimension of 22¾" (24" minus the thickness of both sides). By applying the 1" rule, I'll need one door 23¾" wide or two doors each 11⅞" wide.

The same rule is used for face-frame cabinets as well. Remember to measure the smallest inside dimension. In the case of face-frame cabinets, the dimension is taken from inside stile (vertical face-frame member) face to inside stile face. Then, add 1" and divide by 2 if you need two doors.

12 The door is made from 1¹⁄₁₆"-thick veneer PB. All four edges must have veneer tape applied. Two 35mm holes must be drilled in the door to accept the hidden hinges. They are usually placed 4" from each end and ³⁄₁₆" back from the door edge. A hinge-boring bit in a drill press is the best way to form these holes. To install these hinges perfectly every time, first secure the hinges to the door with their mounting plates attached (use a square to align the hinges at right angles to the door edge). Next, hold the door in its normally open position with a ⅛"-thick spacing stick between the door edge and cabinet face. Drive ⅝"-long screws through the hinge plate and into the cabinet side on both hinges. Once each hinge plate is secured with two screws, detach the hinge from its plate and install the remaining screws. Attach the door and adjust if necessary. I'm using two 107° Blum full-overlay hinges on my door.

13 Build the laminate wood-edge desktop following the instructions detailed in chapter two. Use the dimensions shown in the cutting list for this project.

14 Attach the top to the bookcase end with three 1¼"-long screws. Secure the other end to the printer tower side with screws through the inside of the cabinet. Verify that the top is level. The top surface should be 30⅟₁₆" above the floor.

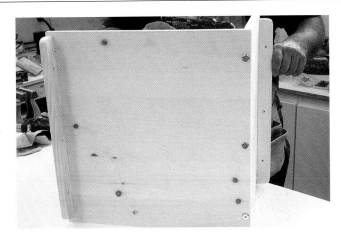

15 The CPU stand is built using 1⅟₁₆" edge-taped veneer PB and two solid wood cleats. Use three screws to attach the boards, and secure the cleats with glue and screws. The cleats should have the outside corners rounded over with a belt sander to avoid injuries if someone bumps against them. One cleat is attached on the top outside face and the other on the bottom board's outside edge.

16 Cut the two adjustable shelf boards (D). Apply wood veneer to one long edge on each board. Then prepare the two side panels (G) and the three fixed shelves (J) by applying wood veneer edge tape to one long edge on each side board and one short edge on each of the fixed shelves. The top fixed shelf is installed flush with the top end of the side boards as shown here, and the bottom fixed shelf with the bottom ends. The middle fixed shelf is attached so its top surface is 24" from the bottom ends of each side panel.

17 Prepare the hutch boards by applying wood veneer edge tape to all front and top edges. Tape all the edges on the backboard, as they will be visible. Secure the sides to horizontal shelves using decorative screws. The lower horizontal shelf's bottom edge should be 8" below each side's top edge. The upper shelf will be 5½" above to leave the proper clearance for both vertical dividers. The backboard is attached flush with the underside of the lower horizontal shelf and even with the sides' top edges. All of the boards can be installed with decorative screws. Divide the shelf into three equal spaces and install the vertical dividers. The hutch can be attached to the tower side with screws through the underside of the desktop on the right-hand side.

18 A commercial plastic pull-out tray is the simplest solution for the keyboard. They're inexpensive, rugged and easy to install. You can also purchase hole grommets for the monitor cables.

armoire work center

An armoire work center addresses many housekeeping problems for the busy home worker. Most importantly, it organizes all your documents and equipment in one place. You don't have to lug everything out each time you begin working — just open the doors and start being productive.

When you have guests drop in, simply close the doors. It's an instant office that's perfect for the bedroom, family room or a large kitchen. And though it's not very difficult to build, this project is one that will be greatly appreciated by any busy home-office worker.

This armoire has large doors with bulletin and memo boards on the back side. There's even a place to hold documents that you need to access quickly and easily.

The adjustable bookshelf is large enough to store CDs, books and directories, and the drawer bank has two utility drawers, as well as a hanging file drawer.

The computer monitor sits directly above a large keyboard tray, and the computer CPU can be mounted on a pull-out tray for easier disk insertion and removal. There's even a place available for storing all of your paper supplies.

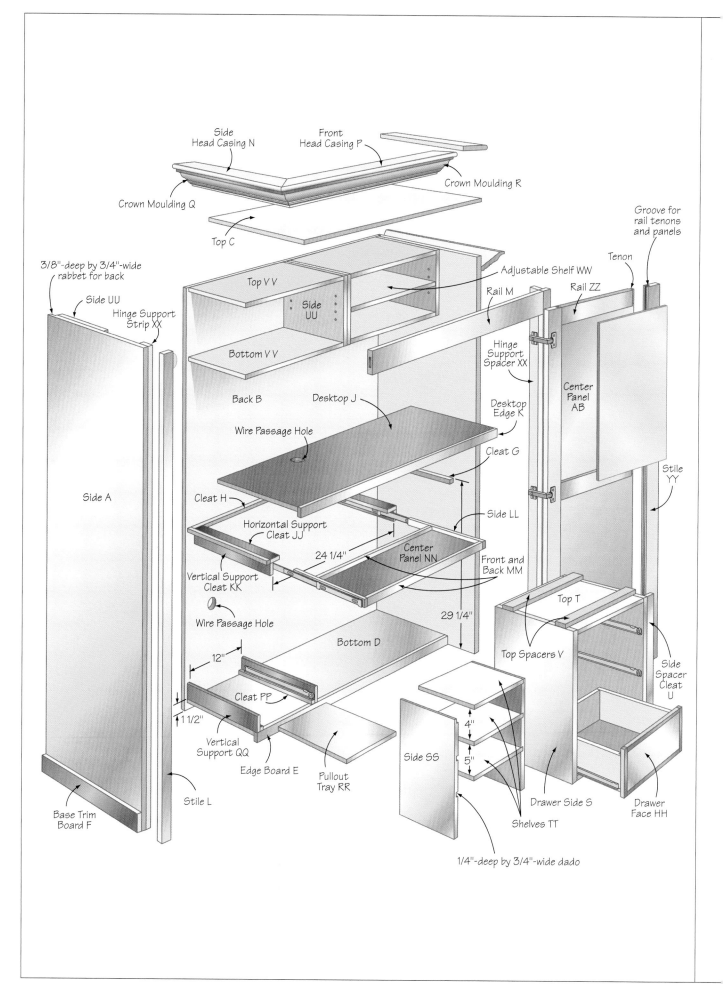

Side Head Casing N

Front Head Casing P

Crown Moulding R

Crown Moulding Q

Top C

Groove for rail tenons and panels

Tenon

3/8"-deep by 3/4"-wide rabbet for back

Side UU

Hinge Support Strip XX

Top V V

Side UU

Adjustable Shelf WW

Rail M

Rail ZZ

Bottom V V

Hinge Support Spacer XX

Center Panel AB

Back B

Desktop J

Wire Passage Hole

Desktop Edge K

Cleat G

Side A

Cleat H

Side LL

Horizontal Support Cleat JJ

24 1/4"

Center Panel NN

Front and Back MM

Vertical Support Cleat KK

Stile YY

Wire Passage Hole

29 1/4"

Top T

Bottom D

Top Spacers V

12"

Cleat PP

Side Spacer Cleat U

1 1/2"

Vertical Support QQ

Side SS

4"

Edge Board E

Pullout Tray RR

5"

Drawer Side S

Drawer Face HH

Base Trim Board F

Stile L

Shelves TT

1/4"-deep by 3/4"-wide dado

REFERENCE	QUANTITY	PART	STOCK	THICKNESS	(mm)	WIDTH	(mm)	LENGTH	(mm)	COMMENTS
A	2	sides	oak plywood	$^3/_4$	(19)	$23^1/_4$	(591)	72	(1829)	
B	1	back	oak plywood	$^3/_4$	(19)	48	(1219)	72	(1829)	
C	1	top	oak plywood	$^3/_4$	(19)	$22^1/_2$	(571)	$47^1/_4$	(1200)	
D	1	bottom	oak plywood	$^3/_4$	(19)	$15^1/_4$	(387)	$47^1/_4$	(1200)	
E	1	bottom edge board	solid oak	$^3/_4$	(19)	$1^1/_2$	(38)	$47^1/_4$	(1200)	
F	2	base trim boards	solid oak	$^3/_4$	(19)	$3^1/_2$	(89)	$23^1/_4$	(591)	
G	2	desktop cleats	solid oak	$^3/_4$	(19)	$^3/_4$	(19)	$45^3/_4$	(1162)	
H	1	desktop cleat	solid oak	$^3/_4$	(19)	$^3/_4$	(19)	$7^7/_8$	(200)	
J	1	desktop	oak plywood	$^3/_4$	(19)	$18^3/_4$	(476)	$47^1/_4$	(1200)	
K	1	desktop edge	solid oak	$^3/_4$	(19)	$1^1/_2$	(38)	$47^1/_4$	(1200)	
L	2	stiles	solid oak	$^3/_4$	(19)	$1^1/_2$	(38)	72	(1829))	
M	1	rail	solid oak	$^3/_4$	(19)	$5^1/_4$	(133)	$45^3/_4$	(1162)	
N	2	side head casing	solid oak	$^3/_4$	(19)	$3^1/_4$	(83)	$26^7/_8$	(683)	angle cut
P	1	front head casing	solid oak	$^3/_4$	(19)	$3^1/_4$	(83)	$53^1/_4$	(1353)	angle cut
Q	2	side crown moulding	solid oak	$^3/_4$	(19)	$3^1/_8$	(79)	$26^1/_4$	(667)	angle cut
R	1	front crown moulding	solid oak	$^3/_4$	(19)	$3^1/_8$	(79)	$53^1/_4$	(1353)	angle cut

DRAWER COMPARTMENT & DRAWERS

REFERENCE	QUANTITY	PART	STOCK	THICKNESS	(mm)	WIDTH	(mm)	LENGTH	(mm)	COMMENTS
S	2	sides	oak plywood	$^3/_4$	(19)	$18^3/_4$	(476)	27	(686)	
T	1	bottom & top	oak plywood	$^3/_4$	(19)	$18^3/_4$	(476)	$17^1/_4$	(438)	
U	1	side spacer cleat	oak plywood	$^3/_4$	(19)	2	(51)	27	(686)	
V	2	top spacers	oak plywood	$^3/_4$	(19)	2	(51)	18	(457)	
W	2	top drawer sides	Baltic birch ply	$^1/_2$	(13)	$4^1/_2$	(114)	18	(457)	
X	2	drawer front & back	Baltic birch ply	$^1/_2$	(13)	$4^1/_2$	(114)	$15^3/_4$	(400)	
Y	1	top drawer bottom	Baltic birch ply	$^1/_2$	(13)	$16^1/_4$	(413)	18	(457)	
Z	2	middle drawer sides	Baltic birch ply	$^1/_2$	(13)	5	(127)	18	(457)	
AA	2	front & back	Baltic birch ply	$^1/_2$	(13)	5	(127)	$15^3/_4$	(400)	
BB	1	middle drawer bottom	Baltic birch ply	$^1/_2$	(13)	$16^1/_4$	(413)	18	(457)	
CC	2	file drawer sides	Baltic birch ply	$^1/_2$	(13)	10	(254)	18	(457)	
DD	2	front & back	Baltic birch ply	$^1/_2$	(13)	10	(254)	$15^3/_4$	(400)	
EE	1	file drawer bottom	Baltic birch ply	$^1/_2$	(13)	$16^1/_4$	(413)	18	(457)	
FF	1	rop drawer face	oak plywood	$^3/_4$	(19)	$6^1/_2$	(165)	$18^1/_2$	(470)	edge w/wood veneer
GG	1	middle drawer face	oak plywood	$^3/_4$	(19)	$6^1/_2$	(165)	$18^1/_2$	(470)	edge w/wood veneer
HH	1	bottom drawer face	oak plywood	$^3/_4$	(19)	$13^1/_2$	(343)	$18^1/_2$	(470)	edge w/wood veneer

KEYBOARD PULL-OUT

REFERENCE	QUANTITY	PART	STOCK	THICKNESS	(mm)	WIDTH	(mm)	LENGTH	(mm)	COMMENTS
JJ	2	horizontal support cleats	oak plywood	$^3/_4$	(19)	$3^1/_4$	(83)	18	(457)	
KK	2	vertical support cleats	solid oak	$^3/_4$	(19)	$3^1/_4$	(83)	18	(457)	
LL	2	sides	solid oak	$^3/_4$	(19)	$1^1/_2$	(38)	18	(457)	
MM	2	front & back	oak plywood	$^3/_4$	(19)	$1^1/_2$	(38)	$21^3/_4$	(552)	
NN	1	center panel	oak plywood	$^3/_4$	(19)	$21^3/_4$	(552)	$12^1/_2$	(318)	

CPU PULL-OUT

REFERENCE	QUANTITY	PART	STOCK	THICKNESS	(mm)	WIDTH	(mm)	LENGTH	(mm)	COMMENTS
PP	2	cleats	solid oak	$^3/_4$	(19)	$^3/_4$	(19)	16	(406)	
QQ	2	vertical supports	solid oak	$^3/_4$	(19)	$3^1/_2$	(89)	16	(406)	
RR	1	pull-out tray	solid oak	$^3/_4$	(19)	11	(279)	16	(406)	

PAPER STORAGE SHELF

REFERENCE	QUANTITY	PART	STOCK	THICKNESS	(mm)	WIDTH	(mm)	LENGTH	(mm)	COMMENTS
SS	2	sides	solid oak	$^3/_4$	(19)	11	(279)	20	(508)	
TT	3	front & back	oak plywood	$^3/_4$	(19)	11	(279)	12	(305)	

REFERENCE	QUANTITY	PART	STOCK	THICKNESS	(mm)	WIDTH	(mm)	LENGTH	(mm)
BOOKCASE									
UU	4	sides	oak plywood	¾	(19)	12	(305)	20	(508)
VV	4	bottom & tops	oak plywood	¾	(19)	12	(305)	22⅛	(562)
WW	2	adjustable shelves	oak plywood	¾	(19)	12	(305)	22	(559)
BOOKCASE									
XX	4	sides	oak plywood	¾	(19)	3	(76)	71¼	(1810)
YY	4	bottom & tops	oak plywood	¾	(19)	3	(76)	67	(1701)
ZZ	2	adjustable shelves	oak plywood	¾	(19)	3	(76)	18⅜	(467)
AB	2	adjustable shelves	oak plywood	¼	(6)	18¼	(464)	30	(762)

HARDWARE AND SUPPLIES

screws

nails

glue

biscuits or dowels

three-quarter extension
drawer glides

full-extension drawer glides
for the file drawer

107° hidden hinges

170° hidden hinges

cable hole grommets

commercial CD racks (optional)

pull-out keyboard tray

drawer and door handles

metal brackets

1 Prepare both side panels by cutting a ¾"-wide by ⅜"-deep rabbet on the inside back edge of each panel. Use a router and straight bit with a guide, or form the rabbet on a router table.

2 The backboard is secured to the two side panels in the rabbet cuts. Use glue and 2" finishing nails driven from the backside of the panel into the side edges.

3 The top board is attached to the sides and backboard with glue and 2" screws. It's installed flush with the top edges of both sides as well as the backboard. The screws can be driven through the side panels because the heads will be covered with trim molding.

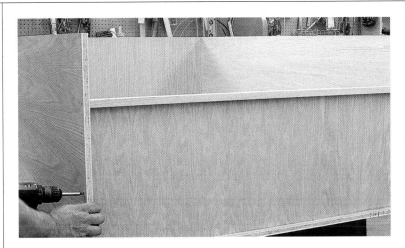

4 | Cut the bottom board to size as detailed in the cutting list. You'll also need to prepare the solid wood strip (E) to cover the front edge on this panel. The edge strip should be rounded over on the front face with a ⅜" roundover bit. Attach it to the bottom board, with its top edge flush with the top surface of the panel, using glue and biscuits or nails. Install the bottom board using glue and 2"-long screws driven through the sides and back panel. The top surface of this board should be 1½" above the bottom edges of the sides and back panels.

5 | The solid wood base trim boards (F) are installed on the lower end of each side panel. Before securing the boards, use a ⅜" roundover bit to remove the top and both end edges. Attach the trim pieces with glue and 1¼" screws. The screw heads are installed under the bottom board, and the trim is clamped only where the screw heads would be visible in front of the bottom board.

6 | Secure the three desktop support cleats (G and H) with glue and 1¼" screws. Predrill the holes in the cleats to avoid cracking the thin strips. Attach the cleats so their top edges are 29¼" above the floor.

7 | The desktop (J) requires a hardwood edge strip (K), similar to the bottom board. Dress the hardwood edge with a ⅜" router bit after attaching it to the desktop. Secure the completed top to the support cleats with glue and 1¼" screws.

Tip

Predrill the holes in each cleat for screws that will be used to support the desktop. The cleats are only ¾" wide and it's difficult to get a drill located correctly after they are installed. Use a bit larger than the screw shaft so the desktop will be tightly drawn to the cleat surface. The screws can only spin freely in the cleats and thread tightly in the underside of the desktop, securing it properly.

8 Cut the bottom board to size as detailed in the cutting list. You'll also need to prepare the solid wood strip (E) to cover the front edge on this panel. The edge strip should be rounded over on the front face with a ⅜" roundover bit. Attach it to the bottom board, with its top edge flush with the top surface of the panel, using glue and biscuits or nails. Install the bottom board using glue and 2"-long screws driven through the sides and back panel. The top surface of this board should be 1½" above the bottom edges of the sides and back panels.

9 The solid wood base trim boards (F) are installed on the lower end of each side panel. Before securing the boards, use a ⅜" roundover bit to remove the top and both end edges. Attach the trim pieces with glue and 1¼" screws. The screw heads are installed under the bottom board, and the trim is clamped only where the screw heads would be visible in front of the bottom board.

11 The desktop (J) requires a hardwood edge strip (K), similar to the bottom board. Dress the hardwood edge with a ⅜" router bit after attaching it to the desktop. Secure the completed top to the support cleats with glue and 1¼" screws.

10 Secure the three desktop support cleats (G and H) with glue and 1¼" screws. Predrill the holes in the cleats to avoid cracking the thin strips. Attach the cleats so their top edges are 29¼" above the floor.

Tip

Now is a great time to sand the face frame smooth. It's also worth taking time to fill the nail head holes before the crown moulding is attached.

13 The drawer compartment contains two utility drawers and a file drawer. Hanging hardware for file folders requires the supports at 15¼" wide. This dimension determines the width of the drawer compartment. The outside dimensions, using ¾"-thick veneer plywood, will be 18¾"-deep by 18¾"-wide by 27"-high. So with that in mind, cut pieces S and T to size and apply wood veneer edge tape to the outside edges. Join the sides to the bottom and top boards using 2" screws and glue. Counterbore the screw holes on the left hand side and fill with wood plugs. The other side will not be visible.

12 Use a ⅜" roundover bit in a handheld router to ease the outside edges of both cabinet stiles. The router will stop at the crown, which will be the endpoint of each cut.

14 Attach the spacer cleat (U) to the right front edge of the compartment using glue and screws. This spacer will provide clearance when opening the drawers. A piece of ¾"-thick plywood veneer will work fine. Secure the two top spacers (V) on the underside of the desktop using 1¼" screws. These spacers will fill the compartment-to-desktop gap. Install the compartment and anchor it with two 1¼" screws through the top and bottom boards.

15 Cut all the pieces of ½"-thick Baltic birch plywood for the three drawer boxes. Each drawer side requires a ½"-wide by ¼"-deep rabbet on both inside ends (refer to the assembly instructions in chapter three when building the draw rs). Then install the bottom-mount drawer glides so there's a 2" space above the file drawer and a 1" space above each utility drawer box. Use 18"-long full-extension drawer glides for the file drawer and 18" bottom-mounted glides for the utility drawers. (I've installed 1½"-wide by ⅛"-thick flat aluminum, ⅜" above the drawer edge, to support the hanging file folders — see chapter ten for more details.)

16   The three drawer faces are made with ¾"-thick veneer plywood. All the edges have iron-on veneer tape to hide the plywood core. The bottom drawer face is installed first and secured flush with the lower edge of the compartment's bottom board. Install the middle face with a 1/16" space between faces. The simplest way to locate drawer faces is to drill the handle hole and drive a screw through that hole into the box. This will secure the face until two 1" screws can be installed through the back of the drawer box front board and into the drawer face.

17   Attach the plywood supports for the keyboard tray to the underside of the desktop with 1¼" screws. Glue and screw the plywood pieces to the solid wood verticals forming two right-angle brackets. Round over the front lower corner on the solid wood supports with a belt sander. Secure the brackets to the desktop so the inside faces of the vertical supports are 24¼" apart.

18   Assemble the keyboard tray as shown. The hardwood side pieces and the front and back strips are secured with glue and screws so they are ¾" above the plywood veneer panel. Counterbore the screw holes and fill with wood plugs. Use a ¼" roundover bit in a router to ease all the hardwood support edges. The tray is fitted with a 18" full-extension drawer glide. The side pieces are 18" long, but the tray platform, including the hardwood front and back rails, is 14" deep. This will provide room at the back of the pull-out for wires from the keyboard, monitor and printer. Mount the drawer glide cabinet members as low as possible on the support brackets.

19   Drill a wire passage hole for a grommet at the back of the desktop. Position the hole near the center of the keyboard pull-out tray. Use a large-diameter grommet to accommodate the large printer cable end. Drill an additional hole under the desktop, through the backboard, for a power supply cord.

20 The CPU pull-out is mounted on 16" bottom-mounted drawer glides. Cut the parts and make the two support brackets as shown. Round over the tops of each upright.

21 Install the CPU pull-out brackets with 1¼" screws driven into the bottom board. Space the inside faces of the vertical members 12" apart. The platform is ¾" veneer plywood with iron-on taped edges. Mount the platform on standard 16" bottom-mounted drawer glides.

22 Build a paper storage compartment using ¾" veneer plywood and apply wood veneer to the front edges. Dado and rabbet the compartment sides and clamp the assembly until the adhesive sets. Edge tape the boards before making the router cuts so the edge veneer will be cut cleanly. This compartment fits between the CPU pull-out and drawer compartment, and does not have to be secured to the armoire carcass.

23 The upper bookcases are two simple boxes with shelf pin holes drilled for adjustable shelving. You must build two boxes, as one full width case cannot be installed in the armoire carcass. Apply wood veneer edge tape to all exposed edges. Join the sides to the bottom and top boards using glue and 2" screws. I installed the cases with 1½"-long screws and decorative washers. I did not glue them in place in case they need to be altered when I purchase new computer equipment.

executive work center

The unique, but simple to build, executive work center has a few hidden design options that will suit almost anyone's needs. The frame-and-panel-style desk has wood compartments that can be fully customized. If you prefer a file drawer in place of the computer processing unit (CPU) cabinet, simply build a different sized box to attach to the desk. The basic desk style remains even though the drawer or door compartments are different.

I've used solid wood legs, ¾"-thick veneer plywood and a solid wood glued-up top. I've also opted to use a full ¾"-thick back on the hutch as well as all the panels. It's a little more expensive, but it's money well invested.

The panel to leg joints give this desk added strength and durability. The full ¾"-thick grooves provide more glue surface and are further strengthened with 2" wood screws.

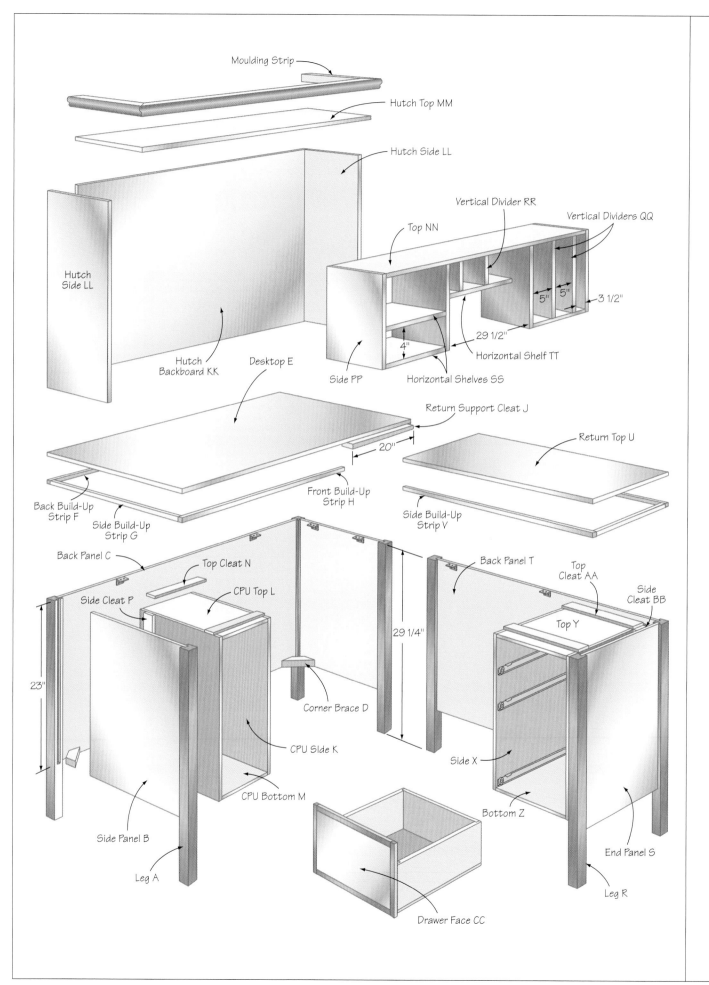

Moulding Strip

Hutch Top MM

Hutch Side LL

Vertical Divider RR

Vertical Dividers QQ

Top NN

Hutch
Side LL

5" 5"

3 1/2"

29 1/2"

4"

Horizontal Shelf TT

Hutch
Backboard KK

Desktop E

Side PP

Horizontal Shelves SS

Return Support Cleat J

Return Top U

20"

Front Build-Up
Strip H

Side Build-Up
Strip V

Back Build-Up
Strip F

Side Build-Up
Strip G

Back Panel C

Top Cleat N

CPU Top L

Back Panel T

Top
Cleat AA

Side
Cleat BB

Side Cleat P

29 1/4"

Top Y

23"

Corner Brace D

CPU Side K

Side X

CPU Bottom M

Bottom Z

Side Panel B

End Panel S

Leg A

Drawer Face CC

Leg R

REFERENCE	QUANTITY	PART	STOCK	THICKNESS	(mm)	WIDTH	(mm)	LENGTH	(mm)	COMMENTS
A	4	desk legs	solid wood	$1^5/_8$	(41)	$1^5/_8$	(41)	$29^1/_4$	(743)	
B	2	desk side panels	oak plywood	$3/_4$	(19)	23	(584)	$25^1/_2$	(648)	
C	1	desk back panel	oak plywood	$3/_4$	(19)	23	(584)	$61^1/_2$	(1562)	
D	2	rear corner braces	solid wood	$1^5/_8$	(41)	$1^5/_8$	(41)	8	(203)	
E	1	desktop	solid wood	$3/_4$	(19)	30	(762)	66	(1676)	make from glued-up boards
F	1	back buildup strip	solid wood	$3/_4$	(19)	$3/_4$	(19)	$64^1/_2$	(1638)	
G	2	side buildup strips	solid wood	$3/_4$	(19)	$3/_4$	(19)	30	(762)	
H	1	front buildup strip	solid wood	$3/_4$	(19)	$3/_4$	(19)	$44^1/_2$	(1130)	
J	1	return support cleat	solid wood	$3/_4$	(19)	$1^1/_2$	(38)	20	(508)	
K	2	CPU sides	oak plywood	$3/_4$	(19)	18	(457)	21	(533)	
L	1	CPU top	oak plywood	$3/_4$	(19)	18	(457)	12	(305)	
M	1	CPU bottom	oak plywood	$3/_4$	(19)	18	(457)	12	(305)	
N	2	CPU top cleats	oak plywood	$3/_4$	(19)	$1^1/_2$	(38)	13	(330)	
P	1	CPU side cleat	oak plywood	$3/_8$	(10)	$1^1/_2$	(38)	21	(533)	
Q	1	CPU door	oak plywood	$3/_4$	(19)	13	(330)	$20^7/_8$	(530)	edged with solid $1/_2$"-thick wood strips
R	3	return legs	solid wood	$1^5/_8$	(41)	$1^5/_8$	(41)	$29^1/_4$	(743)	
S	1	return end panels	oak plywood	$3/_4$	(19)	23	(584)	17	(432)	
T	1	return back panel	oak plywood	$3/_4$	(19)	23	(584)	$37^1/_2$	(953)	
U	1	return top	solid wood	$3/_4$	(19)	$21^1/_2$	(546)	42	(1067)	make from glued-up boards
V	2	side buildup strips	solid wood	$3/_4$	(19)	$3/_4$	(19)	42	(1067)	
W	1	end buildup strip	solid wood	$3/_4$	(19)	$3/_4$	(19)	20	(508)	

DRAWER COMPARTMENT & DRAWERS

REFERENCE	QUANTITY	PART	STOCK	THICKNESS	(mm)	WIDTH	(mm)	LENGTH	(mm)	COMMENTS
X	2	compartment sides	oak plywood	$3/_4$	(19)	18	(457)	21	(533)	
Y	1	compartment top	oak plywood	$3/_4$	(19)	18	(457)	10	(254)	
Z	1	compartment bottom	oak plywood	$3/_4$	(19)	18	(457)	10	(254)	
AA	2	top cleats	oak plywood	$3/_4$	(19)	$1^1/_2$	(38)	$11^1/_2$	(292)	
BB	1	side cleat	oak plywood	$3/_8$	(10)	$1^1/_2$	(38)	21	(533)	
CC	3	drawer faces	oak plywood	$3/_4$	(19)	$6^7/_8$	(175)	11	(279)	edged with solid $1/_2$"-thick wood strips
DD	4	drawer sides	Baltic birch ply	$1/_2$	(13)	$5^1/_2$	(140)	18	(457)	
EE	4	drawer backs/fronts	Baltic birch ply	$1/_2$	(13)	$5^1/_2$	(140)	$8^1/_2$	(216)	
FF	2	drawer bottoms	Baltic birch ply	$1/_2$	(13)	9	(229)	18	(457)	
GG	2	top drawer sides	Baltic birch ply	$1/_2$	(13)	$4^1/_2$	(114)	18	(457)	
HH	2	top drw. backs/fronts	Baltic birch ply	$1/_2$	(13)	$4^1/_2$	(114)	18	(457)	
JJ	1	top drawer bottom	Baltic birch ply	$1/_2$	(13)	9	(229)	18	(457)	

HUTCH & HUTCH DIVIDER

REFERENCE	QUANTITY	PART	STOCK	THICKNESS	(mm)	WIDTH	(mm)	LENGTH	(mm)	COMMENTS
KK	1	back	oak plywood	$3/_4$	(19)	28	(711)	64	(1626)	
LL	2	sides	oak plywood	$3/_4$	(19)	11	(279)	28	(711)	
MM	1	top board	oak plywood	$3/_4$	(19)	$11^3/_4$	(298)	64	(1626)	
NN	1	hutch divider top	oak plywood	$3/_4$	(19)	11	(279)	$62^1/_2$	(1588)	
PP	4	vertical sides	oak plywood	$3/_4$	(19)	11	(279)	12	(305)	
QQ	2	vertical dividers	oak plywood	$3/_4$	(19)	11	(279)	$11^1/_4$	(286)	
RR	2	vertical dividers	oak plywood	$3/_4$	(19)	6	(152)	6	(152)	
SS	3	horizontal shelves	oak plywood	$3/_4$	(19)	11	(279)	15	(381)	
TT	1	horizontal shelf	oak plywood	$3/_4$	(19)	6	(152)	$29^1/_2$	(749)	

HARDWARE AND SUPPLIES

Veneer edge	Tape
Screws	Nails
Glue	Biscuits or dowels

Three-quarter extension drawer glides

Full-extension drawer glides for the file drawer

107° hidden hinges

High-pressure laminate

Contact cement

Cable hole grommets

Commercial CD racks (optional)

Pull-out keyboard tray

Drawer and door handles

Metal brackets

1 Cut the four legs of the desk to size. Two of the legs require a groove that's ¾"-wide by ⅜"-deep by 23"-long on one face measured from the top of the legs. The other two require two grooves of the same size on two adjoining faces of each leg. All the grooves are centered on the leg faces. The grooves are formed with a ¾"-wide straight router bit on a router table. The cut will have a rounded bottom requiring each to be squared so the panels will fit properly.

2 Use a ⅜" roundover bit in a router table to soften the vertical edges on all of the legs. Now is an ideal time to complete the sanding on the legs as the task will be much more difficult after the panels are installed.

4 Install the back panel joining the two desk side assemblies. The panel is secured in the second groove on each back leg and held with glue and screws. Insert these screws, through the leg face opposite the end edges, 2½" from the top and bottom of the back panel on both ends.

3 Attach the side panels to the legs. One double-grooved back leg is at the end of each side panel. Be careful to orient the legs properly so they will receive the back panel. Secure the panels using glue and 2" screws in counterbored holes (they will be filled with wood plugs, through the side opposite each panel edge). Position the screws 2" from the bottom and top edge of each panel.

Cut Once

The legs for the desk and return are prepared in the same manner. Also, note that the panels for both pieces are the same height. To save time and eliminate duplicate set-ups, cut the desk and return legs, as well as the panels, at the same time.

Drill, Don't Split

Always drill a pilot hole for the screw. The screw will cut threads for maximum hold. Without pilot holes the screw shaft is acting like a wedge and could split the material.

5 The two rear corner braces are attached with glue and screws in plugged holes. Before cutting the 45° angle on each end, round over all the edges with a ⅜" bit in a router. Align the sides to the back board at 90° with a carpenter's square before securing the braces. Use 1½"-long screws.

You can create acceptable edges for joining without a jointer. The straight edges can be cut on a table saw as long as the saw is properly aligned. Use the factory edge and cut the opposite side, reducing the width by ¹⁄₁₆". Reverse the board so the cut edge is against the saw fence, and cut another ¹⁄₁₆" off the opposite side. It may be necessary to make more than two cuts but you will achieve an edge that can be joined providing the saw is well-tuned and accurately aligned. Or, if you don't have a biscuit cutter, simple edge-to-edge gluing will also yield an acceptable result. Don't over-tighten the clamps as this will force all the glue out and starve the joint.

6 Join enough solid wood boards to form a top that measures ¾"-thick by 30"-deep by 66"-wide. Joint the edges and use biscuits to create the top. I am using six 1×6 boards to build my top, with biscuits 6" apart.

7 Attach right-angle metal brackets every 6" along the back and two sides of the desk frame. These will be used to secure the top.

8 Once the glued-up top is properly set, trim it to the correct finished size. Install ¾" square build-up strips on the underside, as detailed in the drawing, with glue and finishing nails. The strips are installed flush with the outside edges of the desktop. The edge will be rounded over once the return is attached.

9 Attach the top to the desk base using ⅝" screws through the angle brackets. The top should overhang the legs by 1" on all faces. Don't glue the top in place. This will allow it to move a little during humidity level changes.

| 10 | Cut and install the return support cleat. It should extend ¾" past the front edge of the desktop. Use 1¼" screws to secure the cleat. |

Avoid Bridging

A situation called "bridging" can occur when joining two boards with screws. The threads will run to their ends before both boards are joined tightly leaving a gap in between both. To eliminate this problem, drill a hole larger than the screw diameter in the piece closest to the screw head. The screw will simply rotate in that piece without creating a thread and draw the pieces tightly together. You'll always get tight joints using this technique. Drill larger holes in the return cleat to avoid bridging between the cleat and tops.

| 11 | Apply iron-on wood veneer edge tape to all four front edges of the CPU compartment boards. Join the two sides (K) to the top and bottom boards (L and M) as shown in the illustration. Use glue and 2" screws in counterbored holes that are filled with wood plugs. |

| 12 | Attach the two top cleats on the CPU compartment with glue and finishing nails. The side cleat is ⅜" thick and will fill the gap between the desk leg and side panel. Secure it with glue and finishing nails on the rear left side of the compartment. |

| 13 | Install the CPU compartment, aligning its front edge flush with the face of the desk leg. Use 2"-long screws into the leg, 1½" screws at the back into the side panel, and 2" screws through the top of the compartment into the underside of the desktop. Locate the front screws, which are driven into the leg, 4" on center from the top and bottom of the compartment. The mounting plate of the door hinge will hide them. |

14 Cut a piece of ¾" veneer plywood measuring 12" × 19⅞". Glue and nail ¾"-thick by ½"-high hardwood strips to all edges. Finally, sand and round over the front face edges with a ⅜" router bit. Note: The door for the CPU compartment is made with ¾" veneer plywood and hardwood edge strips. The door width is found by measuring the inside dimension of the compartment and adding 1". The inside dimension is 12", therefore our door width must be 13". The door height for this application covers the top and bottom board edges less ⅛" for desktop clearance. Our finished height is 20⅞". These rules apply when using full-overlay hidden hinges.

15 Drill two 35mm holes on the back of the door that are 4" on center from the top and bottom edges. Install two 110° full-overlay hidden hinges in the holes with the mounting plates attached. Use a ⅛"-thick spacer between the door edge, in its normally open position, and the compartment edge. Hold the door flush with the underside surface of the bottom board and drive screws into the mounting plates (this technique will accurately locate your door).

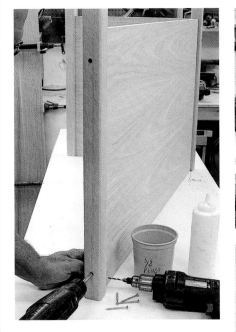

16 Cut the three return legs, and form one groove in two of the legs and two on the third leg. Follow the same procedures as detailed in step one for the desk legs. Cut the side and rear return panels and attach them in the same way the desk panels were installed.

17 The solid wood return top is made following the same steps performed during the desktop construction. However, its finished size is 21½" deep by 42" long.

18 Attach ¾" square build-up strips to the underside of the return top. These are again installed with glue and nails. The return end with one leg is left open so it can be secured to the return cleat on the desk.

19 The top is attached to the return base with right-angle brackets. Then, the return is connected to the desk with screws through the return cleat. Sand the tops smooth and round over the five outside corners to prevent injury. Use a small round object about 1½" in diameter to form identical arcs on each corner. Next, soften the sharp corners with a belt sander.

20 Use a ⅜" roundover bit in a router to remove the sharp edges on both the desk and return top. Round over the bottom and top edges.

22 The drawers are made with ½"-thick Baltic birch plywood. Cut all the parts to size as detailed in the cutting list. Assemble the drawers following the procedures outlined in chapter three. This compartment will hold two 6"-high drawers and one top drawer that is 5" high. Space the 18"-long bottom-mount drawer glides 7" apart beginning at the bottom.

21 Build the drawer compartment following the same procedures as detailed for the CPU compartment. This compartment is a different size and the side cleat is on the right. The drawer compartment is also mounted flush with the front face of the return leg.

23 The drawer faces are made to match the CPU door. Begin with three pieces of ¾"-thick veneer plywood 5⅞" high by 10" wide. Attach ½"-high by ¾"-thick strips on all door edges. Fill the nail holes, sand and round over the front face edges. Install the drawer faces on the boxes with two 1"-long screws through the inside into the drawer face back. Start installing the faces from the bottom; make sure the bottom face is flush with the lower edge of the bottom board. Space the drawer faces 1/16" apart.

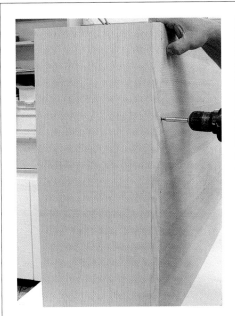

24   The backboards for the hutch's two side edges, which are 28" high, require wood veneer edge tape. The side boards need a 28"-high edge on each covered with veneer. These will be the front edges. Attach the hutch backboard to the side boards with glue and 2" screws. My hutch will be against a wall so the screw heads do not need to be covered.

25   Use glue and 2" screws in counterbored holes to secure the top board (MM) to the sides and back. Fill the holes with wood plugs. The board edges do not have to be covered because a moulding strip will hide them.

26   Install a moulding strip on the front and two side top edges. Choose any moulding that's suitable as long as it's at least ¾" high. Miter the corners at 45° and secure the strip with glue and finishing nails.

27   The divider and compartment section is built as a unit and installed in the hutch. If you wish to use the same design as shown here, cut all the parts to size as detailed in the cutting list. Apply wood veneer edge tape to all exposed edges before joining the boards. The section is assembled using simple butt joints with glue and 2" screws. Remember to counterbore any screw head that will be visible so it can be hidden with a wood plug.

28   Put the divider section into the hutch and secure with 1"-long screws through the top and sides. Counterbore the holes and fill with a wood plug.

student's work center

Children will work better when they have a dedicated, organized area for their projects and homework. Information and the materials needed to work and study are more effectively used when they are within easy reach. To answer these needs, I've designed a work center that may help get them better organized.

The work center is a desk and hutch combination. It provides space for book storage, three large drawers for supplies, and a large work surface made from high-pressure laminate material. This project was made of solid pine and composite veneer board. It's reasonably easy to build and not very expensive. The finish is polyurethane.

To simplify the building process, look at the components: a three-drawer pedestal, a leg, a desktop and a hutch. I've used pine veneer MDF and solid-wood trim. If the desk is too small or large for your space, change the dimensions. The only major difference between this desk and a wider unit is the hutch width. If you need a 30" × 60" desktop, add the extra width onto the horizontal members of the hutch. And if you do have the space for a deeper desktop, consider building the hutch with 1 × 12 lumber.

This project can be matched to the other furniture in this chapter if it will be in the same room. The drawers in this project track on mechanical glides in place of the traditional wood runners. It can be made with wood runners by duplicating the steps used in the other projects, or the others can use mechanical glides. I used the metal glide option here to illustrate the differences; you can decide on the method that works best for you.

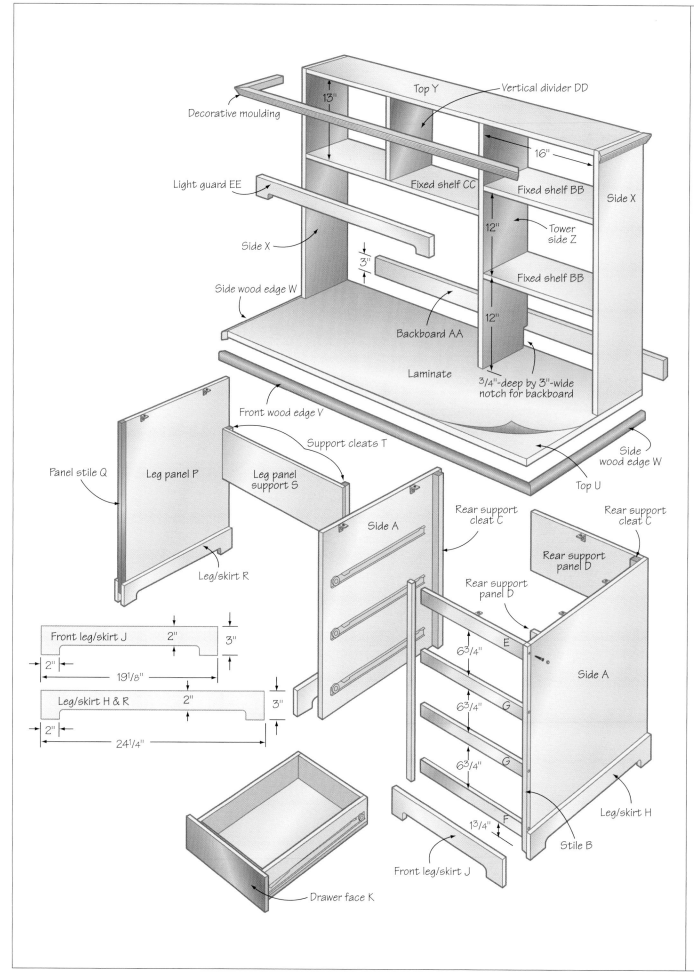

Decorative moulding

Top Y

Vertical divider DD

13"

16"

Light guard EE

Fixed shelf CC

Fixed shelf BB

Side X

Side X

12"

Tower side Z

3"

Fixed shelf BB

Side wood edge W

12"

Backboard AA

Laminate

3/4"-deep by 3"-wide notch for backboard

Front wood edge V

Side wood edge W

Support cleats T

Top U

Panel stile Q

Leg panel P

Leg panel support S

Rear support cleat C

Rear support cleat C

Side A

Rear support panel D

Rear support panel D

Leg/skirt R

Side A

Front leg/skirt J

2"

3"

E

6³/4"

2"

19¹/8"

Leg/skirt H & R

2"

3"

G

6³/4"

2"

24¹/4"

G

6³/4"

Side A

Leg/skirt H

F

1³/4"

Stile B

Front leg/skirt J

Drawer face K

REFERENCE	QUANTITY	PART	STOCK	THICKNESS	(mm)	WIDTH	(mm)	LENGTH	(mm)
DRAWER BANK SECTION									
A	2	sides	veneer MDF	$3/4$	(19)	$23^1/_2$	(597)	$27^1/_2$	(699)
B	2	stiles	solid wood	$3/4$	(19)	$3/4$	(19)	$29^1/_4$	(743)
C	2	rear support cleats	solid wood	$3/4$	(19)	$3/4$	(19)	$27^1/_2$	(699)
D	2	rear support panels	veneer MDF	$3/4$	(19)	7	(178)	16	(406)
E	1	top rail	solid wood	$3/4$	(19)	$2^1/_4$	(57)	16	(406)
F	1	bottom rail	solid wood	$3/4$	(19)	2	(51)	16	(406)
G	2	middle rails	solid wood	$3/4$	(19)	$1^1/_2$	(38)	16	(406)
H	2	legs/skirts	solid wood	$3/4$	(19)	3	(76)	$24^1/_4$	(616)
J	1	front leg/skirt	solid wood	$3/4$	(19)	3	(76)	$19^1/_8$	(486)
K	3	drawer faces	solid wood	$3/4$	(19)	$7^1/_4$	(184)	17	(432)
L	6	drawer sides	Baltic birch	$1/2$	(13)	$5^1/_4$	(133)	22	(559)
M	6	drawer fronts & backs	Baltic birch	$1/2$	(13)	$5^1/_4$	(133)	14	(356)
N	3	drawer bottoms	Baltic birch	$1/2$	(13)	15	(381)	22	(559)
LEG PANEL & SUPPORT									
P	1	leg panel	veneer MDF	$3/4$	(19)	$23^1/_2$	(597)	$27^1/_2$	(699)
Q	1	panel stile	solid wood	$3/4$	(19)	$3/4$	(19)	$29^1/_4$	(743)
R	2	legs/skirts	solid wood	$3/4$	(19)	$3/4$	(19)	$24^1/_4$	(616)
S	1	leg panel support	veneer MDF	$3/4$	(19)	$7^1/_4$	(184)	$29^3/_4$	(756)
T	2	support cleats	solid wood	$3/4$	(19)	$3/4$	(19)	$7^1/_4$	(184)
DESKTOP									
U	1	top	particleboard	$3/4$	(19)	$24^1/_2$	(622)	48	(1219)
V	1	front wood edge	solid wood	$3/4$	(19)	$1^1/_2$	(38)	$49^1/_2$	(1257)
W	2	side wood edges	solid wood	$3/4$	(19)	$1^1/_2$	(38)	$24^1/_2$	(622)
DESK HUTCH									
X	2	sides	solid wood	$3/4$	(19)	$7^1/_4$	(184)	36	(914)
Y	1	top	solid wood	$3/4$	(19)	$7^1/_4$	(184)	$46^1/_2$	(1181)
Z	1	tower side	solid wood	$3/4$	(19)	$7^1/_4$	(184)	$35^1/_4$	(895)
AA	1	backboard	solid wood	$3/4$	(19)	3	(76)	$46^1/_2$	(1181)
BB	2	fixed shelves	solid wood	$3/4$	(19)	$7^1/_4$	(184)	16	(406)
CC	1	fixed shelf	solid wood	$3/4$	(19)	$7^1/_4$	(184)	$29^3/_4$	(756)
DD	1	vertical divider	solid wood	$3/4$	(19)	$7^1/_4$	(184)	13	(330)
EE	1	light guard	solid wood	$3/4$	(19)	4	(102)	$29^3/_4$	(756)

HARDWARE AND SUPPLIES

3 sets–22" (559mm) bottom-mount drawer glides

3–drawer handles

6–right-angle brackets

1 piece–28" x 52" (711mm x 1321mm) high-pressure laminate

6' (2m) decorative moulding

2' (61cm) fluorescent light fixture

wood plugs

finishing and brad nails

wood filler

$5/8$" (16mm) PB screws

1" (25mm) PB screws

$1^1/_4$" (32mm) PB screws

2" (51mm) PB screws

glue

colored putty

$1^1/_2$" (38mm) screws

drawer pulls

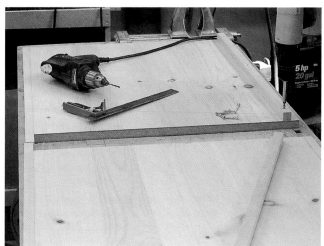

1 Cut the two drawer bank sides A and the leg panel P, as they are all the same size. Each of the three panels requires a ¾" square stile B and Q, which are 29¼" long, applied to one face. Use glue and 2" finishing nails to secure the stiles. Attach each stile so it's flush with the top of the panel. That will make the stile extend 1¾" beyond the panel bottom. Countersink the nail heads and fill the holes with a colored putty to match the final finish.

2 Cut the two rear support cleats C and secure them to the inside face of each drawer bank side A with glue and 1¼" screws. The cleats are attached ¾" in from the back edge of each side. The two drawer bank sides should now be mirror images of each other. The stiles are on the front edges and the cleats on the inside back faces, forming a right and left side.

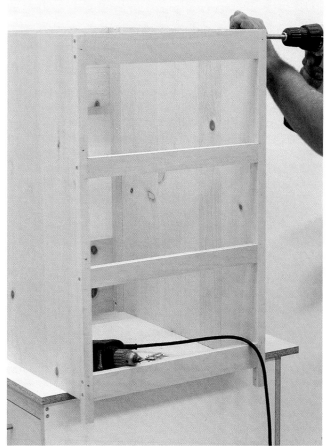

3 Attach the two rear support panels D with screws and glue as shown. These two pieces will not be visible, so any ¾"-thick material will be fine.

4 Install the drawer rails E, F and G as shown in the illustration. Use glue and 2" screws through the stiles B, in pilot holes that have been counterbored to accept wood plugs.

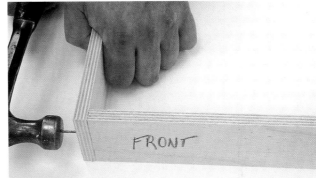

Cutting Patterns

When cutting multiple patterns such as the leg/skirt assemblies, create a pattern with scrap material to use as a guide. Then, after all the pieces are cut, clamp them together and sand the rough edges. This ensures that all the pieces are identical.

---

5 The four side legs/skirt H and R, each 24¼" long, are now required. Cut the pattern as shown in the drawing. Use a ¼" roundover bit in a router to round the top, bottom and back edges on the outside face of each leg/skirt. If you don't own a router, ease the edges with sandpaper. Two will be attached to the drawer bank and two are for the side of the leg panel P. Attach the two legs/skirts H to the drawer bank and legs/skirts R to the leg panel. Use 1¼" screws and glue. The legs/skirts H and R are installed flush with the front face of stiles B and Q and 1¼" up from the bottom edge of the side A and leg panel P.

6 The front leg/skirt J is 19⅛" long and cut as shown in the drawing. All edges of the face side should be rounded over. Attach the board using 1¼" screws and glue, aligning it to the side legs/skirts H. Three screws will hold the board securely until the adhesive cures. I cut it a little longer to provide a slight overhang on both sides so that the ends can be sanded flush to the side legs/skirts H after installation.

7 The bottom-mount drawer glides I used required a ½" space per side for proper operation. Therefore, my drawer box is 1" narrower than the opening. Normally, my drawer box height is also 1" less. The drawer sides, back and front are made from Baltic birch plywood. The drawer bottom can be ½" Baltic birch or ¼"-thick plywood; either is acceptable. Cut all the drawer box parts as detailed in the materials list and sand the edges smooth. Then join the sides L to the front and back M, using glue and finishing nails or 1½"-long screws.

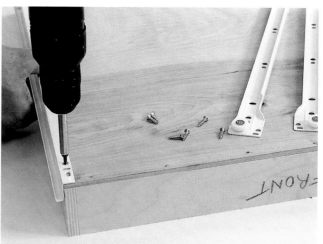

8   The drawer bottom N is attached using glue and finishing nails. The bottom should be cut square and aligned to all faces of the drawer box. If it is square and aligned, your drawer box will be square.

9   Install the 22" bottom-mount drawer glides by first attaching the runners to the drawer box.

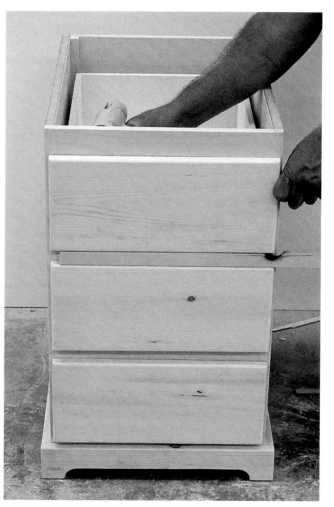

10   Use a carpenter's square to draw a line ¾" up from each rail to make a screw hole line for the two cabinet runners of each drawer glide set.

11   Make the three drawer faces K using 1×8 lumber. Trim to the size indicated and round over all edges of the outside face with a ¼" router bit. Attach the drawer faces with 1" screws through the drawer box. Each face should overlap its top and bottom rail by ¼".

Mounting Drawer Fronts

Mounting drawer fronts accurately can be difficult. But here is an easy method. First, drill the handle holes in the drawer face only. Then, hold the drawer face in position and drive screws through the handle holes into the drawer box.

Remove the drawer with the face attached and secure the face from the rear. Finally, remove the screws, complete drilling the holes through the drawer box, and install your handle hardware. You'll have perfectly aligned faces every time!

13 Begin building the desk hutch by joining the two sides X to the top Y. Use glue and 2" wood screws. The screw heads will be covered by trim moulding, so they can be driven flush with the side surfaces.

12 To complete the drawer bank, install right-angle brackets around the top edge. These will be used to secure the desktop.

14 Cut the tower side Z to the dimensions shown in the materials list. Before installing, notch the bottom back edge for the backboard AA. Secure the tower side Z to the top Y, using 2" wood screws in piloted counterbored holes that can be filled with wood plugs. Install the tower side Z leaving a 16" space for the fixed shelves BB.

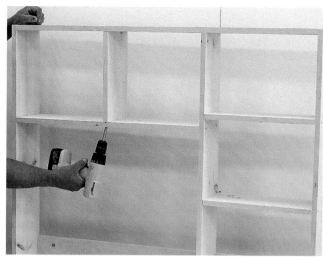

15 Backboard AA is installed to strengthen the hutch and is attached to the sides X and tower side Z with screws and glue. Fill the holes on the outside faces of the sides X with wood plugs.

16 Attach the fixed shelves BB and CC, and vertical divider DD with glue and 2" wood screws. Fill the holes with plugs. Shelf spacing and the number of fixed shelves required depend on your storage needs. Customize this section to suit your requirements.

17 If you plan to install a 2' fluorescent lamp under the long shelf, the optional light guard EE, cut in the same style as the legs/skirt, will conceal the fixture. It's attached with glue and screws through the sides X and Z, as well as the top of the long fixed shelf CC.

18 Erase all the front edges of the hutch with a ¼" roundover bit in a router, with the exception of the top Y. If you plan to install 1"-high decorative moulding as I've done, stop the roundover procedure at a point where the moulding crosses the hutch's vertical boards. This will provide a square flat surface to attach the decorative moulding.

19 Choose a suitable decorative moulding for the top of the hutch. Secure it with glue and brad nails. You'll need about 6' of moulding and a miter box to cut the 45° corners.

Building the Desktop

The desktop for this project is made with a ¾"-thick particleboard or plywood substrate. Wood edges are attached to the front and two sides of the substrate. Then a high-pressure laminate is glued to the substrate, using contact cement. Finally, the laminate is trimmed and rounded over with a router bit. Follow the procedures detailed in project one of chapter two to make your wood-edged laminate desktop.

You'll need a ¾" top U 24½" deep by 48" long. The front wood edge V is a ¾"-thick by 1½"-high solid piece of wood 49½" long. The two side wood edges W are the same height and thickness and are 24½" long.

The laminate material should be about 28" × 52". It's larger than the top, but you'll need a little extra material because it's difficult to align. The overhang can be cut with a flush-trim router bit. High-pressure laminates are an excellent choice for this desktop as they provide a smooth writing surface that will handle a great deal of abuse.

Assembling the Work Center

From this point forward, all the assembly will be done using screws. Glue should not be used in case the desk needs to be taken apart for moving or you need to replace the desktop due to wear or damage.

Attach the leg panel assembly to the drawer bank case using leg panel support S. The leg panel support S is held in place by the two support cleats T — one on the leg panel P and the other attached to the drawer bank side. Secure it with 1¼" wood screws about midpoint on each assembly. Then, install two right-angle brackets on leg panel P so it can be attached to the underside of the desktop. Set the desktop on the drawer bank and leg panel. Secure the top to the drawer bank and leg panel with ⅝"-long screws in the right-angle brackets.

Place the hutch on top of the desk. Align the backboard AA with the back edge of the desktop. Install two 2" wood screws from the underside of the desktop into the backboard AA to secure it in place. Install the drawers and verify all the components fit and operate properly. Once the test fitting is complete, take the assemblies apart and apply a finish.

office bookcase

There's always a need for extra book storage in the office. Although we depend heavily on computers, we still require those invaluable reference books.

I made this project using oak veneer plywood and solid woods. The shelves are all adjustable, and I've used a little different technique for the supports in place of the usual holes. These metal shelf standards are installed in a groove, are capable of handling heavy loads and are available in a number of finishes. I used white so it would be easier to see in the photographs; however, gold might be more suitable with the natural clear polyurethane that I've applied. The choice is up to you but is often determined by the final color of the bookcase. One note: Purchase your shelf standards before cutting the grooves. There are size variations depending on the manufacturer, and you want to be sure the cut is correct.

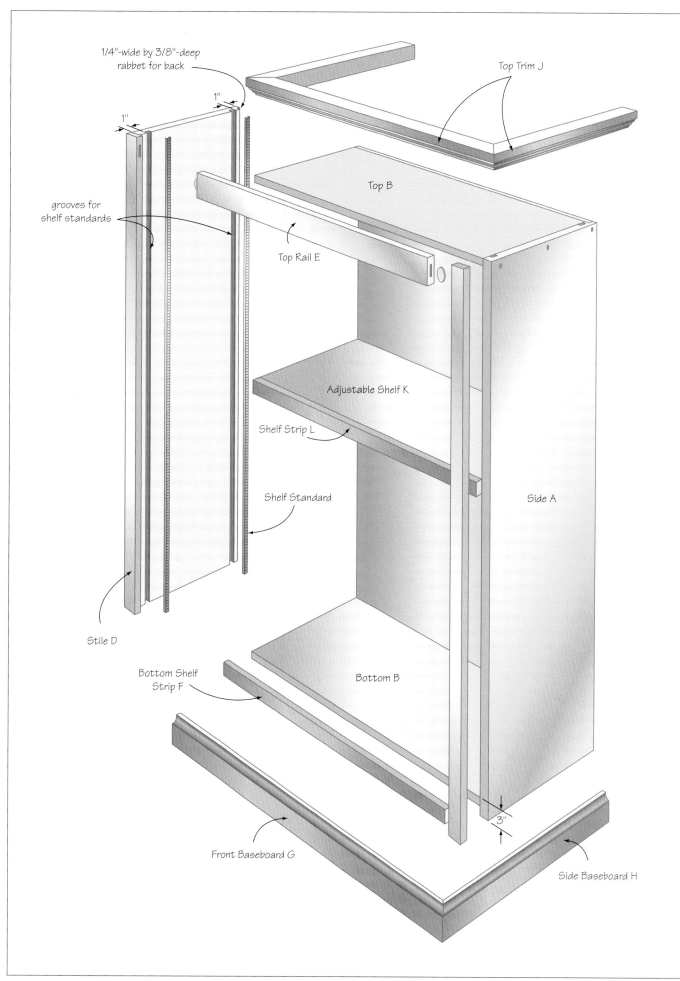

1/4"-wide by 3/8"-deep rabbet for back

1"

1"

Top Trim J

grooves for shelf standards

Top B

Top Rail E

Adjustable Shelf K

Shelf Strip L

Stile D

Shelf Standard

Side A

Bottom Shelf Strip F

Bottom B

3"

Front Baseboard G

Side Baseboard H

REFERENCE	QUANTITY	PART	STOCK	THICKNESS	(mm)	WIDTH	(mm)	LENGTH	(mm)	COMMENTS
A	2	sides	oak plywood	$^3/_4$	(19)	$11^7/_8$	(302)	78	(1981)	
B	2	top and bottom	oak plywood	$^3/_4$	(19)	$11^7/_8$	(302)	$31^3/_4$	(806)	
C	1	back	oak plywood	$^1/_4$	(6)	$32^1/_2$	(826)	$75^3/_4$	(1924)	
D	2	stiles	solid wood	$^3/_4$	(19)	$1^1/_2$	(38)	78	(1981)	
E	1	top rail	solid wood	$^3/_4$	(19)	$3^1/_2$	(89)	$30^1/_4$	(768)	
F	1	bottom shelf strip	solid wood	$^3/_4$	(19)	$1^1/_2$	(38)	$30^1/_4$	(768)	
G	1	front baseboard	solid wood	$^3/_4$	(19)	3	(76)	$34^3/_4$	(883)	bevel cut on both ends
H	2	side baseboards	solid wood	$^3/_4$	(19)	3	(76)	$13^1/_2$	(343)	bevel cut on one end
J	7'	top trim	solid wood	*		*		*		depends on style chosen
K	4	shelves	oak plywood	$^3/_4$	(19)	$10^7/_8$	(276)	$31^1/_2$	(800)	
L	4	shelf strips	solid wood	$^3/_4$	(19)	$1^1/_2$	(38)	$31^1/_2$	(800)	

HARDWARE AND SUPPLIES

glue

screws

shelf standard

adjustable shelf pins

biscuits or dowels

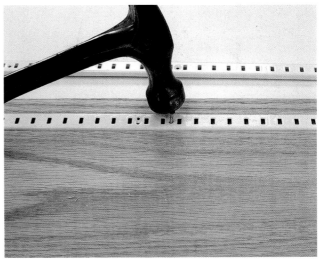

 Each side (A) requires a rabbet on the rear inside face that's $^3/_8$" wide by $^1/_4$" deep. They also need two grooves 1" in from the edges, for the shelf standards.

2 The shelf standards should be cut 78" long. Install them in the grooves and use the small nails provided to secure the standards.

4   Use glue and brad nails to attach the backboard. Take a little extra time to cut the back accurately because a squarely cut back will properly align the bookcase carcass.

3   Attach the two sides to the top board with glue and 2" screws (it should be flush with the upper ends of the sides). Drive the screws through the outside face on the side panels, as they will be covered with trim. Attach the bottom board in the same way, aligning its top surface 3" above the bottom ends of the sides. The top and bottom boards should be flush with the side boards' front edges.

5   Attach the stiles flush with the outside face of each side board. There are a number of methods you can use to attach the stiles. Glue and clamps, glue with biscuits, or simply glue and face nailing with finishing nails are all acceptable. I used the glue-and-face-nail method and filled the nail holes with colored wood filler to match my final finish. Install one stile at this time. Attach the other side after the upper rail is secured.

Adding Some Interest

You can add a little interest and change the appearance of your bookcase by cutting flutes in the stile faces. A V-bit installed in a router can create an interesting pattern. The cut depth controls flute width.

6 The upper rail is installed with biscuits into the side of each stile. Additionally, apply glue to the edge of the carcass top board and face nail the rail. After the rail is secured, install the remaining stile.

7 Attach the hardwood strip (F) to the front edge of the bottom shelf. This will extend the bottom shelf making it flush with the stile faces. Glue and nail the strip in place and don't be concerned about filling the nail head holes as they will be covered by the base trim.

Working with Mouldings

The top moulding can be purchased or made with a router bit. There are dozens of possible patterns. If you make a lot of trim moulding for your projects, a moulding head cutter for the table saw, such as the Magic Molder from LRH Enterprises Inc., is a worthwhile investment.

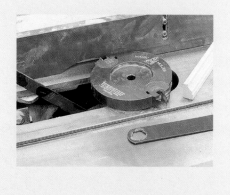

8 The base trim measurements in the cutting list are taken at the longest point of the 45° angle cuts. The top edge of the trim is decorated with a cove bit in a router. Attach the baseboards with glue and 1¼" screws on the backside. These trim boards should be installed flush with the top surface of the bottom board.

9 Before installing the top trim, round over the inside edges of the two stiles and top rail with a ⅜" roundover bit. The router base plate will be stopped by the base trim and determines the point at which the roundover stops on each stile.

10 Cut the three pieces of top trim moulding at 45°. Use the dimensions in the cutting list as a guide — verify the measurements on your bookcase before cutting the trim to size. Use glue and nails to attach the moulding.

Rout First, then Cut your Miters

You'll get "cleaner"-looking corners on trim boards, with decorative router cuts, by routing the design patterns before mitering the corners. This technique prevents routing mistakes when trying to cut a pattern near a mitered end.

11 Before standing the bookcase upright, round over the outside edges of both stiles. Use a ⅜" roundover bit in a router. The upper and lower trim boards will stop the router travel and determine the cut length.

12 Cut the four shelf boards (K). The front trim pieces (L) for the shelves will make them appear thicker and add a great deal of strength to the boards. Use glue and nails or biscuits to attach the edges. Round over the top and bottom with a ⅜" roundover bit.

Construction Notes

I've finished my bookcase with three coats of semi-gloss polyurethane. The first coat was cut with 10 percent mineral spirits and sanded with 320-grit papers. The final full-strength coat was rubbed with paste wax and extra-fine steel wool.

The design options for this project are numerous. I've mentioned a few with regards to trim style and fluted stiles. But there are the more common changes such as width and height variations to suit your needs. If you plan on loading the shelves with extra-heavy items, add a hardwood strip on the back edge.

Veneer plywood is an excellent choice for this project because of its strength. MDF and solid wood panels are also worth considering.

This bookcase is a simple project and will be one of the most appreciated in your home office.

lateral file cabinet

This lateral file cabinet has two drawers that have been sized to store legal file folders, but they can be reduced in depth if you need to store letter-sized folders instead. It will be used in a home office setting with the executive work center in chapter six and the credenza and bookcase hutch in chapter seven. I've used the same simple finish on all three pieces — three coats of oil-based polyurethane.

Since I plan on using hanging file folders, I've come up with a simple track system using aluminum flat stock. You can use a commercial version, but I've found the flat stock setup to be stronger and less expensive.

The small base raises the cabinet off the floor. For most rooms, this will work fine. However, since there's a heating vent where I want to place my cabinet, I added four wheels. Your cabinet can be built either way. In fact, you can eliminate the 1½"-high base completely and attach the wheels directly to the bottom.

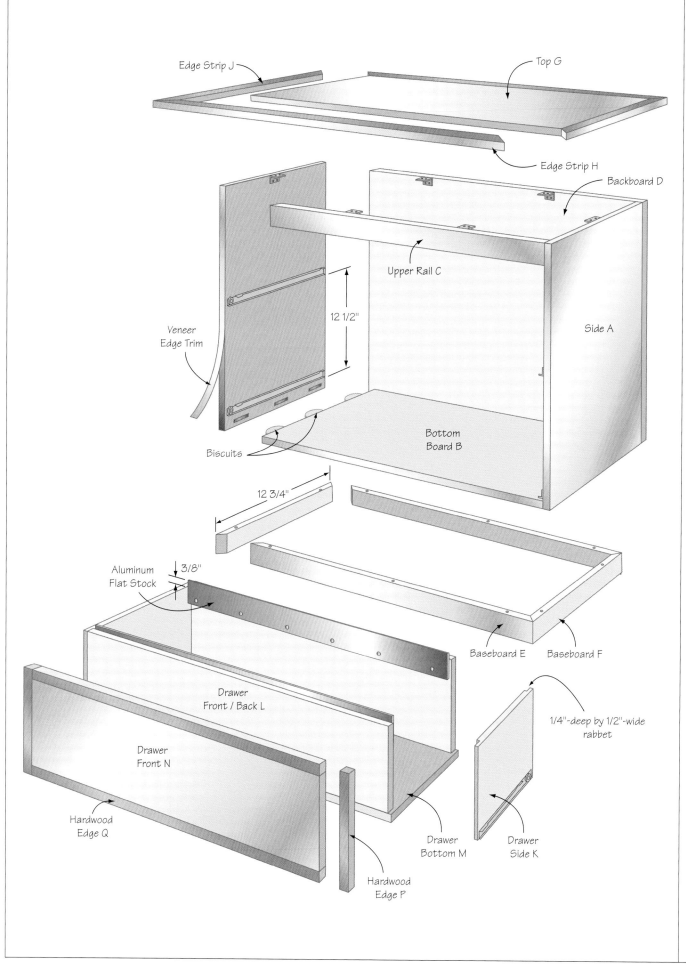

Edge Strip J

Top G

Edge Strip H

Backboard D

Upper Rail C

12 1/2"

Veneer
Edge Trim

Side A

Biscuits

Bottom
Board B

12 3/4"

Aluminum
Flat Stock

3/8"

Baseboard E   Baseboard F

1/4"-deep by 1/2"-wide
rabbet

Drawer
Front / Back L

Drawer
Front N

Hardwood
Edge Q

Drawer
Bottom M

Drawer
Side K

Hardwood
Edge P

Screws

full-extension drawer glides

drawer handles

wheels (optional)

nails

glue

aluminum flat bar stock

REFERENCE	QUANTITY	PART	STOCK	THICKNESS	(mm)	WIDTH	(mm)	LENGTH	(mm)
A	2	sides	veneer PB	$^{11}/_{16}$	(17)	$16^{1}/_{2}$	(419)	$27^{3}/_{4}$	(705)
B	1	bottom board	veneer PB	$^{11}/_{16}$	(17)	$16^{1}/_{2}$	(419)	38	(965)
C	1	upper rail	veneer PB	$^{11}/_{16}$	(17)	2	(51)	38	(965)
D	1	back	veneer PB	$^{11}/_{16}$	(17)	$39^{3}/_{8}$	(1000)	$27^{3}/_{4}$	(705)
E	2	baseboards	solid wood	$^{3}/_{4}$	(19)	$1^{1}/_{2}$	(38)	$35^{1}/_{4}$	(895)
F	2	baseboards	solid wood	$^{3}/_{4}$	(19)	$1^{1}/_{2}$	(38)	$12^{3}/_{4}$	(324)
G	1	top	veneer PB	$^{11}/_{16}$	(17)	$15^{1}/_{2}$	(398)	38	(965)
H	2	top edge strips	solid wood	$^{3}/_{4}$	(19)	1	(25)	38	(965)
J	2	top edge strips	solid wood	$^{3}/_{4}$	(19)	1	(25)	$15^{1}/_{2}$	(394)
FILE DRAWERS									
K	4	sides	birch ply	$^{1}/_{2}$	(13)	10	(254)	$16^{1}/_{8}$	(410)
L	4	front/back	birch ply	$^{1}/_{2}$	(13)	10	(254)	$36^{1}/_{2}$	(927)
M	2	drawer bottom	birch ply	$^{1}/_{2}$	(13)	$16^{1}/_{8}$	(410)	37	(940)
N	2	drawer front	veneer PB	$^{11}/_{16}$	(17)	12	(305)	38	(965)
P	4	drawer edges	hardwood	$^{11}/_{16}$	(17)	$^{1}/_{2}$	(13)	12	(305)
Q	4	drawer edges	hardwood	$^{11}/_{16}$	(17)	$^{1}/_{2}$	(13)	39	(991)

1 Cut the two sides (A) and apply wood veneer iron-on edge tape to one long edge on each panel. These finished edges will be the fronts.

2 The bottom board (B) also requires one long edge be taped. Trimming some wood veneers, such as oak, can be difficult. The wood grain is wide and the tape can split along the fibers. To prevent this, use a router equipped with a flush-trim bit. Be sure to hold the router flat on the board and the edge will be perfect.

Tip

These drawers can be quite heavy when fully loaded, so be careful when they're fully open. I plan on securing my cabinet to a wall stud with a 3" screw. You might want to consider doing this as well for an added measure of safety.

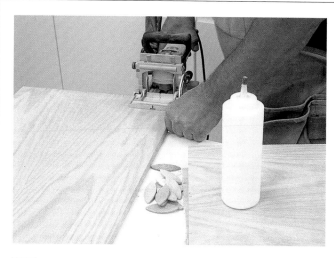

3 | The sides are joined to the bottom board using glue and screws, dowels or biscuits. I've decided to use biscuits for my project.

4 | Tape one long edge on the upper rail. This will be the downside or exposed edge of the rail. It's attached with glue and a right-angle bracket on each end. The rail face is flush with the outside edges of the sides and even with their tops.

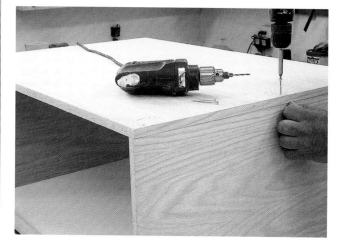

5 | I use a full ¹¹⁄₁₆"-thick back on this cabinet because of the potential weight in the drawer. Before installing, tape the two outside vertical edges with veneer tape. The back is applied with glue and screws, dowels or biscuits. I am using screws because the back will be against a wall and therefore not visible. If the back of your cabinet is exposed, use dowels or biscuits and glue. You can use screws but the holes must be counterbored and filled with wood plugs or buttons.

6 | Construct the base with 1×2 solid wood. The corners are mitered at 45° and secured with glue and brad nails.

Tip

For projects using ¹¹⁄₁₆" or ¾" sheet goods, which are to be joined with biscuits, I always use a No. 10 biscuit. The No. 20 setting may cut too deep and there is a possibility the outside of the board can be punctured.

7 | Clamp the base in place on the underside of the bottom board. It should be 2" in from all edges of the cabinet. Trace its position and drill holes through the bottom board. Apply glue to the base and set the frame in place. Using the previously drilled holes as references, drill pilot holes into the base from the top side of the bottom board. Secure the frame to the bottom board with two 1½" screws on the back, front and two sides.

8 | The top is made with an $^{11}/_{16}$"-thick veneer PB center and framed with 1½"-wide hardwood. The hardwood frame measurements are given for the inside-to-inside 45°-angled cut on each piece.

9 | Secure the wood edge strips to the top board using No. 20 biscuits and glue. After checking the fit, cutting the biscuit slots and applying glue, clamp the assembly together until the adhesive sets.

10 | Sand the top smooth, being careful not to damage the veneer layer. Round over the top and bottom edges with a ⅜" roundover bit.

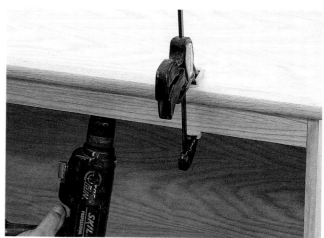

11 Install right-angle brackets on the top edge of the cabinet. These will be used to secure the top board with ⅝" screws.

12 Clamp the top in place so it's flush with the backboard and equally overhanging on each side. Use ⅝" screws through the brackets into the underside of the top.

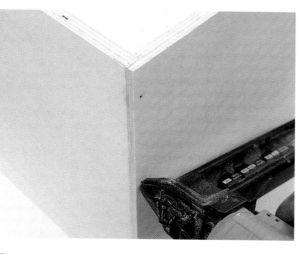

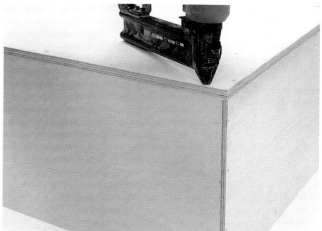

13 Cut the drawer boards using ½"-thick Baltic birch plywood. Glue and nail the sides to the front board and backboard.

14 The drawer bottoms are attached in the same manner. Take the time to cut each bottom board square. Attaching a board with 90° angles to a box will force it into square.

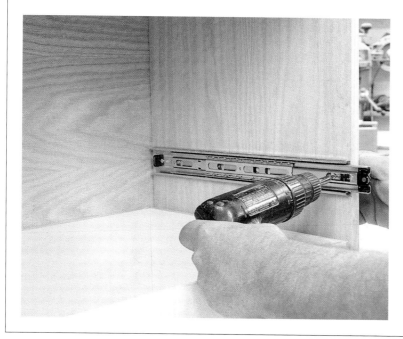

15 The 16" drawer glides should be the full-extension type so files can be easily and fully accessed. Side-mounted glides from Accuride or bottom-mounted hardware from Blum are two examples of the hardware I use. Install the glides according to the manufacturer's instructions, leaving a 2" space between the top edge of the bottom drawer and the bottom of the top drawer.

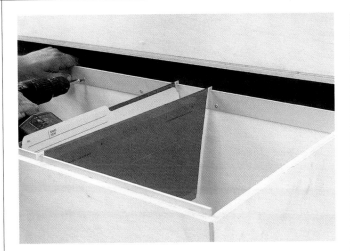

16 Install a 36"-long by 1½"-wide by ⅛"-thick piece of aluminum flat stock on the inside of each front and back drawer board. This flat stock can be purchased at most hardware stores. The metal is secured with ⅝"-long screws in countersunk holes drilled in the flat stock. Each strip should be ⅜" above the drawer edge so the hanging folders can slide freely along the track.

17 Glue and nail the hardwood edge strips for the drawer faces in place. I used simple butt joints at each corner; however, they can be cut at 45° to match the top if you wish. Then sand the faces smooth, taking care not to sand through the wood veneer. Use a ⅜" roundover bit to soften the outside edges on each drawer face. Locate and drill the drawer handle holes in the drawer face only. Align the bottom drawer face flush with the underside of the bottom board. Use 2" screws driven through the handle holes into the drawer box to secure the face temporarily. Open the drawer and drive a 1" screw into the drawer face from the inside of the drawer box at each corner. Finally, remove the screws in the handle holes and complete the drilling so the handles can be installed. Repeat the process for the top drawer face, leaving ¹⁄₁₆" between the two faces.

Construction Notes

As mentioned in the introduction, I finished my cabinet with three coats of oil-based polyurethane. However, the veneers and solid wood will look great with a stain or water-based clear coat. If you plan on painting your file cabinet, consider using the less expensive poplar veneers and solid wood or MDF.

The wood-edged top and drawer faces are another area that can be modified. Use the wood-edged laminate method, such as was detailed in chapter two, if you want a unique pattern. The GP laminates are very tough and will stand up to more abuse than wood veneers.

You can also opt for a solid wood top. They are made by edge gluing boards, using biscuits. The solid wood tops are beautiful and durable.

The cabinet width, as well as its height and number of drawers, are easily modified to suit your needs. If you have different subjects in your file system, you may want three 24"-wide drawers to better separate the information. The construction methods are the same no matter what design you choose.

The hanging file folders I found in my local stationery store appeared to be all the same width. However, before building the cabinet I suggest you check the folders in your area. I don't suspect they would be different but it's worth the time to be sure.

And finally, the cabinet can be mounted on the 1½"-high base or on wheels as I mentioned in the introduction. The base height is variable and doesn't affect any other dimension. If you live in an older home with high baseboards, you might want to alter the size. If the baseboard frame clears the trim it will allow the cabinet to sit tightly against a wall. By doing that, the cabinet-to-wall gap is eliminated and you won't have papers falling off the back.

stand up desk

If you think better on your feet, then you definitely need this desk. You can put your foot on the front rail and get really comfortable. The two drawers have pencil holders and plenty of room for paper storage. The top has a faux leather panel that provides a nice writing surface. The stool provides a place to sit if you want to rest your feet.

This design is not new. Many of our United States founding fathers used this style of desk. If you have a bad back, sometimes standing feels better than sitting. Also, it was fun to build a matching stool.

I like legs that taper so that the legs become larger at their bottoms. It makes the project look more solid. The curved rails and rungs lighten the look of the pieces. You may choose to make this desk out of walnut or cherry. The darker woods will add a bit of "formality" to the desk, perhaps making it more suitable for your needs.

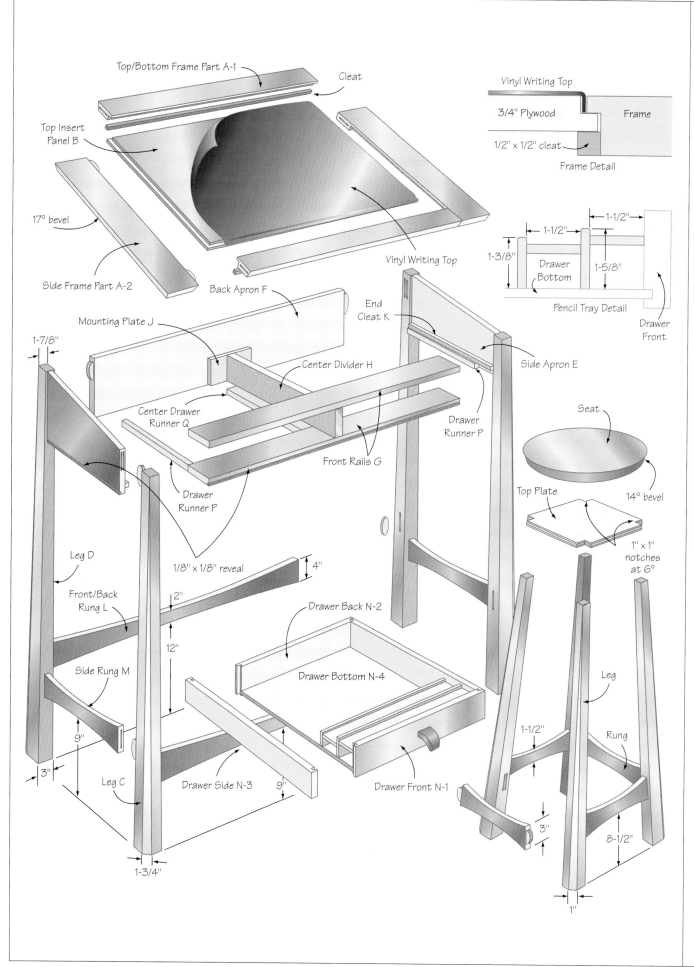

Top/Bottom Frame Part A-1

Cleat

Top Insert Panel B

17° bevel

Side Frame Part A-2

Vinyl Writing Top

3/4" Plywood

Frame

1/2" x 1/2" cleat

Frame Detail

Vinyl Writing Top

Back Apron F

End Cleat K

Mounting Plate J

Center Divider H

Side Apron E

1-1/2"

1-1/2"

1-3/8"

Drawer Bottom

1-5/8"

Pencil Tray Detail

Drawer Front

1-7/8"

Center Drawer Runner Q

Front Rails G

Drawer Runner P

Seat

Top Plate

14° bevel

Drawer Runner P

1" x 1" notches at 6°

Leg D

1/8" x 1/8" reveal

4"

Front/Back Rung L

2"

Drawer Back N-2

Side Rung M

12"

Drawer Bottom N-4

Leg

Rung

9"

3"

Leg C

Drawer Side N-3

9"

Drawer Front N-1

1-1/2"

3"

8-1/2"

1-3/4"

1"

REFERENCE	QUANTITY	PART	STOCK	THICKNESS	(mm)	WIDTH	(mm)	LENGTH	(mm)	COMMENTS
A	1	top	ash	$1^1/_4$	(32)	$23^1/_2$	(597)	38	(965)	
A-1	2	top/bottom frame parts	ash	$1^1/_4$	(32)	3	(76)	28	(711)	
A-2	2	side frame parts	ash	$1^1/_4$	(32)	5	(127)	$23^1/_2$	(597)	
B	1	top insert panel	birch ply	$3/_4$	(19)	$18^1/_2$	(470)	29	(737)	
C	2	front legs*	ash	3	(76)	3	(76)	42	(1067)	each leg tapers to $1^7/_8$" at the top
D	1	back legs*	ash	3	(76)	3	(76)	44	(1118)	each leg tapers to $1^7/_8$" at the top
E	2	side aprons	ash	1	(25)	5	(127)	$17^3/_4$	(451)	see illustration for details
F	1	back apron	ash	1	(25)	7	(178)	$32^1/_4$	(819)	
G	1	front rails	ash	1	(25)	4	(102)	$33^1/_4$	(845)	attach to back end of center divider
H	2	center divider	ash	1	(25)	$2^5/_8$	(68)	$19^1/_4$	(489)	
J	2	mounting plate	plywood	$3/_4$	(19)	3	(76)	3	(76)	
K	2	end cleats	ash	$7/_8$	(22)	$7/_8$	(22)	$17^1/_2$	(445)	
L	1	front/back rungs	ash	1	(25)	4	(102)	$32^1/_4$	(819)	
M	2	side rungs	ash	1	(25)	4	(102)	$17^3/_4$	(451)	
N	1	drawers	ash	$2^5/_8$	(68)	$15^5/_8$	(397)	$19^1/_4$	(489)	
N-1	2	fronts	ash	$3/_4$	(19)	$2^5/_8$	(68)	$15^5/_8$	(397)	
N-2	1	backs	ash	$1/_2$	(13)	$2^5/_8$	(68)	$15^1/_8$	(384)	
N-3	1	sides	ash	$1/_2$	(13)	$2^5/_8$	(68)	19	(483)	
N-4	2	bottoms	birch ply	$1/_4$	(6)	$15^1/_8$	(384)	$18^3/_4$	(476)	
P	2	drawer runners	ash	1	(25)	1	(25)	$43^1/_2$	(1105)	
Q	2	center drawer runner	ash	1	(25)	3	(76)	$18^1/_2$	(470)	
R	1	pencil tray bottoms	ash	$1/_4$	(6)	$1^1/_2$	(38)	$23^1/_4$	(591)	
S	2	pencil tray front	ash	$1/_4$	(6)	$1^3/_8$	(35)	$23^1/_4$	(591)	
T	2	pencil tray center	ash	$1/_4$	(6)	$1^5/_8$	(41)	$23^1/_4$	(591)	
U	2	drawer pulls	padauk	$3/_4$	(19)	1	(25)	$1^1/_4$	(32)	any contrasting wood will work; see illustration for details

HARDWARE AND SUPPLIES

vinyl writing top $1/_{16}$" x 20" x $30^1/_2$"

screws

glue

biscuits

contact cement

*The legs are tapered on the two outside sides only. The inside sides ar left square for ease of assembly.

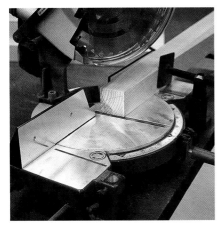

1. First, machine the legs using the tapering jig on the table saw. Since the tops of the legs are angled to match the pitch of the work surface, move over to the miter saw and cut the leg tops to the appropriate angle as shown here.

2. Plane off the outside corners of the legs at a taper to add a lighter look and feel to the desk. You can do this with either a jointer or with a hand plane. The taper width at the bottom of the leg can be adjusted to whatever looks and feels right to your personal taste.

3. To draw the curve of the rungs, begin by marking the width at the center of the piece. Then simply connect the two corners with the center mark by bending a strip of wood and tracing the line as shown here.

4   If you don't have a doweling jig, a homemade jig is easy to make. The front rails are doweled to the front legs because biscuits wouldn't work. In this photo, the jig is referenced to the edge of the end of the rail with a block attached to the jig.

5   In this photo, the reference block is removed and the edge of the jig is set on a pencil mark drawn where the edge of the rail will go.

6   Assemble the top frame using biscuits. Be sure to set them back far enough so they won't show through when the angle on the edge of the top is cut.

7   Glue up the rails, aprons, legs and rungs. Then attach the center divider, side runners and bottom runners. Take your time and make sure these parts all line up and are parallel to each other so that the drawers fit well.

Detail showing the left apron and rear leg joint. The 1/8" × 1/8" reveal at the bottom of the apron adds a nice shadow line.

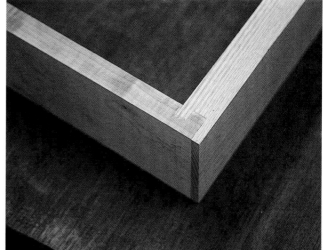

8   Assemble the drawers as detailed in the tech art and cutting list. Pay particular attention to the locking mortise-and-tenon joint used at the front of the drawers (shown here). This joint is made using the table saw. Again, take your time and cut test pieces to get the fit just right.

9 Add the drawer pulls of your choice. Here, I used hand-carved pulls with the tool marks still showing to add texture and character.

10 After cutting the stool legs to size as per the cutting list, glue and screw them to the stool top plate. Note that the notches are cut at the same angle as the tops and bottoms of the legs.

12 Cut the seat to size. To create the bevel, use a band saw with its table tilted at an angle. Then attach the seat to the top plate.

11 Mark the rungs for the stool in the same way you did for the desk. Then cut to shape. Remember that the ends of the rungs are cut at the same angle as the leg ends.

13 Construct the writing panel using the same methods as for the previous project. Attach it to the assembly with cleats and screws. Then finish the desk with three coats of clear catalyzed lacquer. A coat of wax on the drawer sides and the runners will let the drawers slide in and out smoothly.

Task Light

When sanding, it helps to have a task light set up to create sharp shadows on the work. All imperfections can be seen and sanded out.

writing desk

Sometimes you need a quiet place to sit and write that letter or novel. This desk is based on the style of a roll top desk. It gives the feeling of privacy with the wrap-around sides and has plenty of drawers and cubbyholes to keep things organized. The faux leather top creates a perfect writing surface. The top also opens up to reveal a pencil holder and room for storing writing paper inside.

The tapered legs "anchor" the desk to the floor, which gives it a solid look. I've always preferred legs with this taper as opposed to legs with a taper where the legs get narrower at their bottoms, which makes a table or desk look top heavy.

An option to the lift-up top is a lap drawer (see Stand Up Desk project for drawer-making details). You may find it more convenient to open a drawer when the desktop is piled with your work papers.

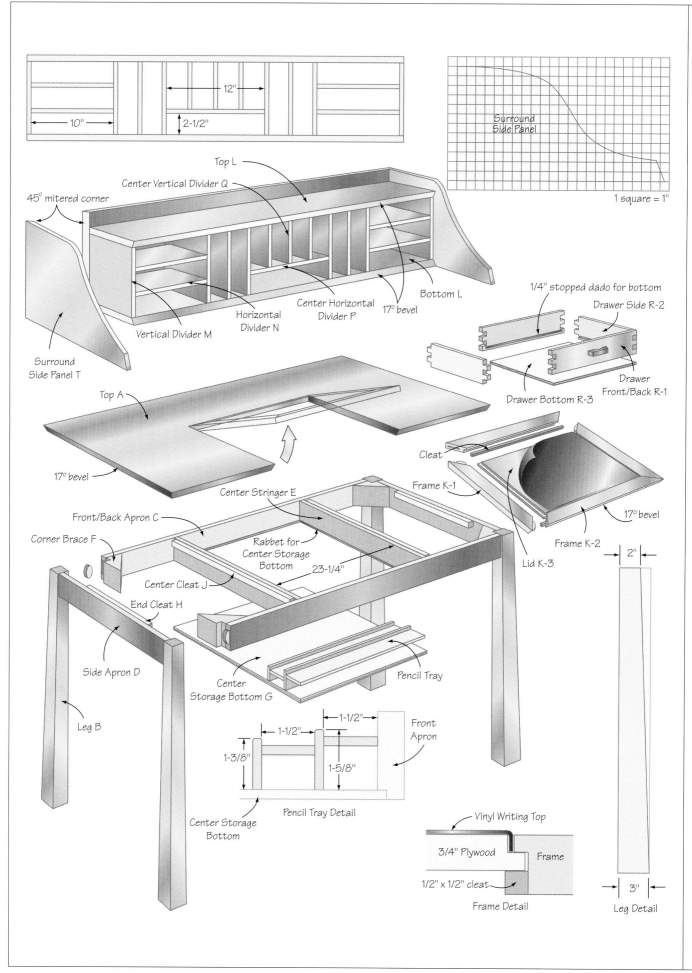

12"

10"

2-1/2"

Surround Side Panel

1 square = 1"

45° mitered corner

Top L

Center Vertical Divider Q

1/4" stopped dado for bottom

Drawer Side R-2

Surround Side Panel T

Vertical Divider M

Horizontal Divider N

Center Horizontal Divider P

17° bevel

Bottom L

Drawer Bottom R-3

Drawer Front/Back R-1

Top A

17° bevel

Center Stringer E

Front/Back Apron C

Corner Brace F

Rabbet for Center Storage Bottom

Center Cleat J

End Cleat H

23-1/4"

Cleat

Frame K-1

Lid K-3

Frame K-2

17° bevel

2"

Side Apron D

Center Storage Bottom G

Pencil Tray

Leg B

1-1/2"

1-1/2"

1-3/8"

1-5/8"

Front Apron

Center Storage Bottom

Pencil Tray Detail

Vinyl Writing Top

3/4" Plywood

Frame

1/2" x 1/2" cleat

Frame Detail

3"

Leg Detail

REFERENCE	QUANTITY	PART	STOCK	THICKNESS	(mm)	WIDTH	(mm)	LENGTH	(mm)	COMMENTS
A	1	top	walnut	$1\frac{1}{4}$	(32)	28	(711)	48	(1219)	w/24"-wide by 18"-deep opening
B	4	legs*	walnut	3	(76)	3	(76)	$28\frac{1}{2}$	(724)	each leg tapers to 2" at the top
C	2	front/back aprons	walnut	$\frac{7}{8}$	(22)	3	(76)	$41\frac{1}{2}$	(1054)	
D	2	side aprons	walnut	$\frac{3}{4}$	(19)	3	(76)	$21\frac{1}{2}$	(546)	
E	2	center stringers	walnut	3	(76)	3	(76)	$23\frac{3}{4}$	(603)	
F	4	corner braces	walnut	$1\frac{3}{4}$	(45)	3	(76)	5	(127)	
G	1	center storage bottom	birch ply	$\frac{1}{2}$	(13)	24	(210)	$24\frac{1}{2}$	(622)	
H	2	end cleats	poplar	$\frac{7}{8}$	(22)	$\frac{7}{8}$	(22)	$15\frac{1}{2}$	(394)	
J	2	center cleats	poplar	$\frac{7}{8}$	(22)	$\frac{7}{8}$	(22)	$23\frac{1}{2}$	(597)	
K	1	lid	walnut	$1\frac{1}{4}$	(32)	$17\frac{7}{8}$	(454)	$23\frac{15}{16}$	(608)	
K-1	2	led frame sides	walnut	$1\frac{1}{4}$	(32)	$1\frac{1}{2}$	(38)	$17\frac{7}{8}$	(454)	
K-2	2	lid frame top/bottom	walnut	$1\frac{1}{4}$	(32)	$1\frac{1}{2}$	(38)	$23\frac{15}{16}$	(608)	
K-3	1	lid panel	walnut	$\frac{3}{4}$	(19)	$16\frac{3}{8}$	(416)	$22\frac{7}{16}$	(570)	

*The legs are tapered on the two outside sides only. The inside sides are left square for ease of assembly.

REFERENCE	QUANTITY	PART	STOCK	THICKNESS	(mm)	WIDTH	(mm)	LENGTH	(mm)	COMMENTS
L	2	top/bottom	walnut	$\frac{3}{4}$	(19)	8	(203)	$45\frac{3}{4}$	(1162)	
M	8	vertical dividers	walnut	$\frac{1}{2}$	(13)	$7\frac{1}{2}$	(191)	$8\frac{1}{2}$	(216)	
N	4	horizontal dividers	walnut	$\frac{1}{2}$	(13)	$7\frac{1}{2}$	(191)	10	(254)	
P	1	center horizontal divider	walnut	$\frac{1}{2}$	(13)	$7\frac{1}{2}$	(191)	12	(305)	
Q	3	center vertical dividers	walnut	$\frac{1}{2}$	(13)	$7\frac{1}{2}$	(191)	$5\frac{1}{2}$	(140)	
R	6	drawers	walnut	$2\frac{1}{2}$	(64)	10	(254)	$7\frac{3}{8}$	(188)	
R-1	6	fronts/backs	walnut	$\frac{1}{2}$	(13)	$2\frac{1}{2}$	(64)	$9\frac{9}{16}$	(243)	
R-2	12	sides	walnut	$\frac{1}{2}$	(13)	$2\frac{1}{2}$	(64)	$7\frac{3}{8}$	(188)	
R-3	6	bottoms	walnut	$\frac{1}{4}$	(6)	$6\frac{13}{16}$	(173)	$9\frac{1}{2}$	(242)	
S	1	surround back	walnut	$\frac{3}{4}$	(19)	12	(305)	$47\frac{1}{4}$	(1200)	
T	2	surround side panels	walnut	$\frac{3}{4}$	(19)	12	(305)	$22\frac{1}{2}$	(572)	
U	2	pencil tray bottoms	walnut	$\frac{1}{4}$	(6)	$1\frac{1}{2}$	(38)	$23\frac{1}{4}$	(590)	
V	1	pencil tray front	walnut	$\frac{1}{4}$	(6)	$1\frac{3}{8}$	(35)	$23\frac{1}{4}$	(590)	
W	1	pencil tray center	walnut	$\frac{1}{4}$	(6)	$1\frac{5}{8}$	(41)	$23\frac{1}{4}$	(590)	
X	6	drawer pulls	padauk	$\frac{1}{2}$	(13)	$\frac{3}{4}$	(19)	2	(51)	any contrasting wood will work

HARDWARE AND SUPPLIES

vinyl writing top $\frac{1}{16}$" x $17\frac{1}{2}$" x $23\frac{1}{2}$"

18mm Soss hinges (2)

screws

glue

biscuits

contact cement

2 Mark the tops of the legs with an orienting triangle. This is a great aid in keeping the legs in proper order.

3 Using double biscuits increases the joint strength significantly.

1 Use a tapering jig to put the taper on the legs. This homemade jig can be adjusted to make a variety of tapers. (Note the two adjusting screws that make it easy to change the amount of taper.)

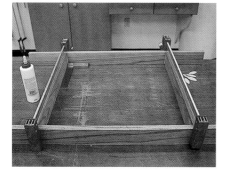

4 After routing a small bevel on the bottom outside edge of the aprons. Glue up the assembly of the two long apron pieces and the two stringers.

5 Cut a rabbet in the glued-up assembly for the bottom piece of the storage area.

6 Glue the two end apron/leg assemblies together first. Then glue the two end assemblies together. Use the scrap wedge-shaped pieces that fell off when cutting the leg tapers as shims to square the clamp faces to the assembly.

7   After cutting the corner blocks to size on a miter saw, go to the table saw and cut notches in the corner blocks for the legs. This can also be done either with a handsaw or on the band saw.

8   Glue the corner blocks in place. These blocks add strength to the leg/apron corner assemblies.

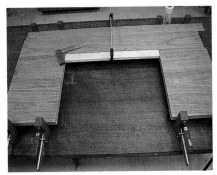

9   After gluing cleats to the aprons and stringers for attaching the top to the base, drill ¼" pilot holes in the cleats for screwing the top to the base. These oversize holes will let the screws move with the solid wood top.

10   Make the top in three pieces (this makes it easy to create the opening for the lid). Double-check for squareness. Cut the angle on the top's edge using a table saw or a circular saw.

11   Attach the top with washers and screws. The washers help to keep the screws from pulling into the cleats.

Tip

The upper desk organizer has several cubbyholes and six openings for the drawers. Take your time laying out this assembly and draw lines where all the parts will go. Using biscuits to assemble this organizer will make it easier to line everything up at assembly time. By laying the top and bottom out at the same time, it is easy to see where all the parts will go.

12 Attach the storage area bottom with screws. You can leave the rabbet corners rounded or square them out. Either way will look good.

13 On a table saw, cut the rabbet on the lid frame stock. Then cut the stock to length as indicated in the cutting list and glue the parts together. Use biscuits in the corner joints for strength.

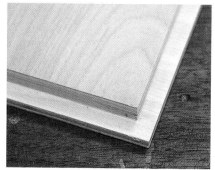

14 Cut a ¾" birch (or any smooth veneer) plywood panel to fit exactly in the opening of the desk lid. Then cut a rabbet on all the edges of the panel so it fits into the top frame opening of the lid. Make sure that the top surface of the panel is flush to the top surface of the frame. Allow for the thickness of the faux leather material around the edges of the top opening. Attach the vinyl to the panel with contact cement. Roll it out smoothly, starting in the center of the panel and working out to the edges, so no bubbles occur.

15 Trim the vinyl so there is a flap left all around the edges of the panel lip. This flap will fold into the opening of the frame when the panel is installed. Cut a notch in the vinyl at the corners so it will fold properly.

16 The panel can then be pushed into the lid opening from the inside of the frame and the vinyl will fold into the rabbet.

17 Secure the panel in place with cleats. The cleats can be removed if the top material needs to be replaced.

18 Attach the lid to the desk. I used invisible Soss hinges, but a brass continuous hinge would also look great. Finally, sand all the parts, finishing up with 150-grit sandpaper. This project was finished with three coats of catalyzed lacquer. A wipe-on finish containing Danish or tung oil and polyurethane would work very well also. Sand with 320-grit sandpaper between coats. Rub out the final coat with #0000 steel wool.

20 Use cardboard to mock-up the shape of parts so you can see what they will look like. This gives you the freedom to change any shape very easily. Then use the cardboard mock-up as a pattern to make a routing template from ¼" plywood.

19 The desktop organizer is assembled using biscuit joinery. Dry fit the desktop organizer to be sure it will all come together properly. Then glue the two drawer opening sections and the center assembly together first, and then the whole organizer (you may want to finish all the parts first, then glue it all together).

Cutting Box-Joint Fingers

After setting up the dado stack cutters to cut a ⅜"-wide by ⅜"-deep notch, make the first cut in the miter-gauge fence. Cut a piece of wood the exact size of the dado cut in the fence and put it in the slot with part of it sticking out past the face of the fence. Move the fence over the exact width of the dado cut. This will give you the proper spacing for cutting the fingers.

Place a spacer the same width of the finger against the spacing block and make the first cut. Note the sandpaper attached to the miter fence to help hold the pieces firmly in place.

Move the piece until the spacing block is in the slot you just cut and make the second cut.

Repeat this step for the final cut.

Place the edge of the side against the spacer block and make the first cut.

Move the side piece over and drop the side over the spacer block into the cut just made and make the final cut.

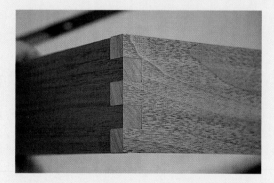

This is what the assembled joint will look like when all of the fingers are cut.

21   When the surround parts are cut, lay the parts flat with the miters facing down. Butt the edges of the miters to each other and tape the joints together using clear packaging tape. Carefully turn the assembly over, apply glue in the miter joint and fold it into a right angle. Stand the surround assembly up and let the glue dry completely before moving it. (You might need to use a large bar clamp at the front edges to pull the assembly square.)

22   Now it's time to glue up the pencil holder.

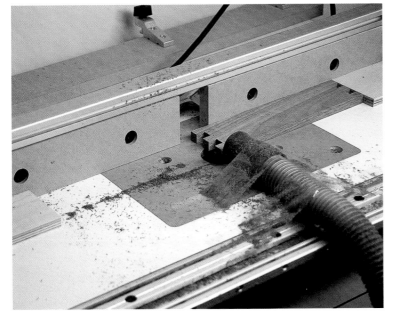

23   Cut a stopped dado for the drawer bottom in the front and back pieces. This dado is cut all the way through on the side pieces. Note the plywood stop blocks that regulate the length of the dado.

24   Fit the drawers with a belt sander.

tall display cabinet

I built this cabinet using oak veneer multi-core plywood and solid wood. However, it can be made with any wood that matches your décor.

The lights, glass shelves and glass panel door combine to make this a beautiful and functional cabinet. The high cost of glass can be an important consideration, so I suggest you call your local glass supplier for a quote before starting this project.

Biscuit joinery is used extensively in this project. It's the ideal choice when joining solid wood to sheet material. If you haven't invested in a biscuit joiner, you're missing out on a great tool.

The glass panel door was built using a mortise-and-tenon joint, and the glass panels have been set in a rabbet and secured with wood strips.

One of the best features of this project is the glass shelves. They can be adjusted to suit any collection, but more importantly, they allow the lights to illuminate every part of the cabinet.

This project can be built with or without a door. The cabinet looks and functions beautifully either way. The door offers an extra degree of security and provides more dust protection for your valuables.

The beauty and function of this cabinet is obvious when used to display collectibles, such as these Capodimonte figures, which are owned by the author.

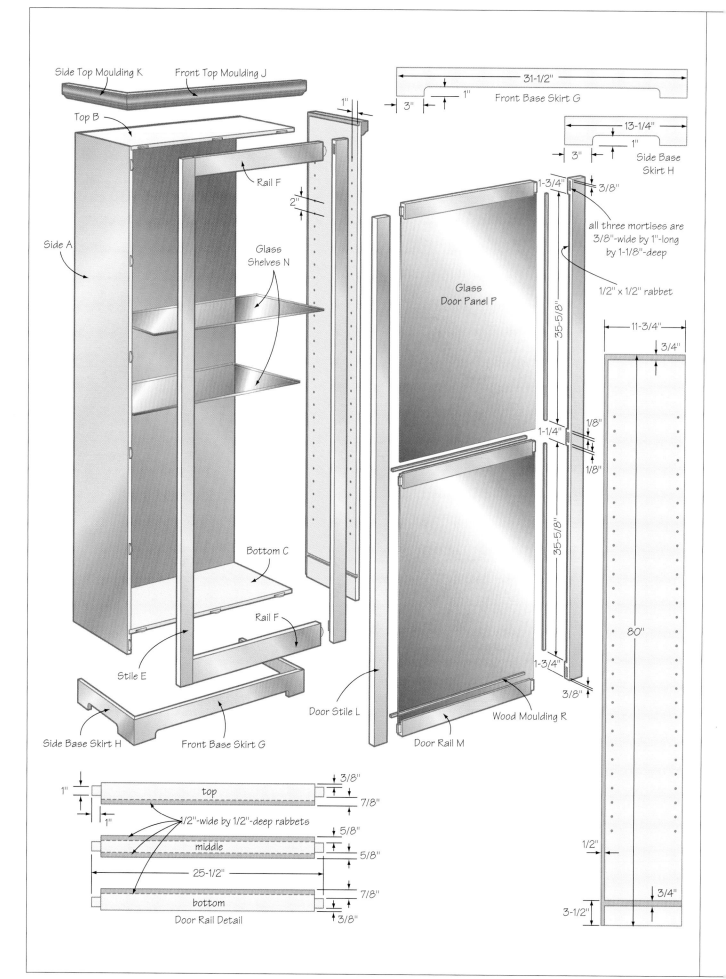

Side Top Moulding K

Front Top Moulding J

Top B

Side A

Rail F

2"

1"

1"

Glass Shelves N

Bottom C

Rail F

Stile E

Side Base Skirt H

Front Base Skirt G

Door Stile L

Door Rail M

Wood Moulding R

Glass Door Panel P

31-1/2"

Front Base Skirt G

1"

3"

13-1/4"

1"

3"

Side Base Skirt H

1-3/4"

3/8"

all three mortises are 3/8"-wide by 1"-long by 1-1/8"-deep

1/2" x 1/2" rabbet

35-5/8"

1-1/4"

1/8"

1/8"

35-5/8"

1-3/4"

3/8"

11-3/4"

3/4"

80"

1/2"

3/4"

3-1/2"

Door Rail Detail

1"

3/8"

7/8"

top

1"

1/2"-wide by 1/2"-deep rabbets

5/8"

middle

5/8"

25-1/2"

7/8"

bottom

3/8"

REFERENCE	QUANTITY	PART	STOCK	THICKNESS	(mm)	WIDTH	(mm)	LENGTH	(mm)	COMMENTS
A	2	sides	oak plywood	3/4	(19)	11 3/4	(298)	80	(2032)	
B	1	top	oak plywood	3/4	(19)	11 1/4	(286)	29 1/2	(749)	
C	1	bottom	oak plywood	3/4	(19)	11 1/4	(286)	29 1/2	(749)	
D	1	back	oak PB	1/2	(13)	29 1/2	(749)	77 1/4	(1962)	
E	2	stiles	oak	3/4	(19)	1 1/2	(38)	80	(2032)	
F	2	rails	oak	3/4	(19)	3 1/2	(89)	27	(686)	
G	1	front base skirt	oak	3/4	(19)	3	(76)	31 1/2	(800)	miter cut both ends
H	2	side base skirts	oak	11/16	(18)	3	(76)	13 1/4	(337)	miter cut one end
J	1	front top moulding	oak	11/16	(18)	1	(25)	31 1/2	(800)	miter cut both ends
K	2	side top mouldings	oak	11/16	(18)	1	(25)	13 1/4	(337)	miter cut one end
L	2	door stiles	oak	3/4	(19)	2 1/4	(57)	75	(1905)	
M	3	door rails	oak	3/4	(19)	2 1/4	(57)	25 1/2	(648)	
N	5	shelves	glass	1/4	(6)	11	(279)	28 3/8	(721)	tempered w/polished edges
P	2	door panels	glass	1/8	(3)	24 3/8	(619)	35 1/8	(892)	
Q	4	wood mouldings	oak	3/8	(10)	3/8	(10)	36	(914)	rough length
R	4	wood mouldings	oak	3/8	(10)	3/8	(10)	25	(635)	rough length

HARDWARE AND SUPPLIES

20 shelf pins for glass shelves

3 European hinges

1 Prepare the two sides A by cutting the dadoes and rabbets as shown in the diagram. Use a ½" router bit in a table or with a guide bar if you're cutting the joints with a handheld router. Note that the rabbet on top, as well as the dado for the bottom shelf, is ½" wide. The back edge rabbet is only ½" wide.

2 Drill two columns of holes on the inside face of each side panel for the adjustable shelf pins. Purchase the pins before drilling the holes to determine the exact size required. Make a jig with scrap lumber, spacing the holes about 2" apart. Drill the hole columns 1" in from each edge.

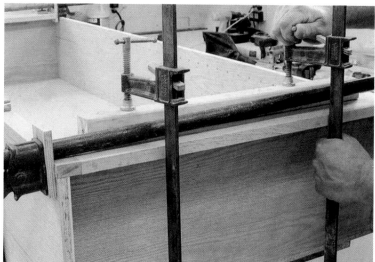

3 | Cut and install the top and bottom boards B and C. They are attached flush with the front edges of each side. The top board can be glued and nailed in place because trim will cover the nail holes. The bottom board C must be attached with glue applied to the dadoes and clamped until set.

4 | I used ½"-thick veneer particleboard in place of the normal ¼" back board to add strength to this tall cabinet. Apply glue to the rabbets and nail the panel from the back side. Be sure to cut this board accurately so it will square the cabinet when installed.

5 | one stile E flush with the outside face of the side panel. It can be attached with glue and nails, or with glue and biscuits.

6 | the upper and lower rails F using glue and biscuits. Use one biscuit to secure each rail to the stile and three more to attach them to the top and bottom boards. The top edge of the bottom rail should be flush with the top surface of the bottom board.

7   Now install the remaining stile E with glue and biscuits. Attach it so its outside edge is flush with the outside face of the side board. If you don't own a biscuit joiner, attach the stiles and rails with glue and nails or dowels.

8   The base skirt consists of three pieces, G and H, as detailed in the Materials List. They are joined with 45° miters at each corner. Before cutting the miters, use a cove bit in your router to detail the top edge of each piece. Cutting the cove detail before the miters results in crisp corners on the skirt. Cut the pattern as shown and sand smooth.

9   Attach the three skirt boards to the case. The top edge of the skirt boards is secured 1¾" above the bottom edge of the side boards. Apply glue and attach the boards using 1¼" screws. Drive two screws into the back of each side skirt and four into the front skirt board.

10   The top moulding J and K can be any style. Pick a pattern that matches the furniture in the room where this case will be used. I've chosen a pattern that matches the cove detail on the skirt boards. Use glue and brad nails to secure the moulding.

11   Use a ⅜"-radius roundover bit in a router to ease the outside corners of each stile L. The router will stop when it hits the upper trim and lower skirt, determining the cut length.

Tip

The door is 28"-wide by 75"-high. It will overlap the top and bottom rail by 1". The overlap design determines the door height. The door width, when using European or hidden hinges, can be easily calculated for this or any other cabinet. Measure the interior dimension of the cabinet and add 1" to that figure. That is the width of a door for this cabinet. If you require two doors, simply divide the calculated inside measurement by 2. For example, the inside measurement of this cabinet is 27". By adding 1" to the dimension I'll need one 28"-wide door or two 14"-wide doors.

12 Prepare the door stiles by cutting two rabbets ½"-wide by ½"-deep in each one. Stop the rabbets 1¾" from each end and leave a 1¼" uncut area at the center of each rail, M. The rabbets can be cut with a straight bit in a router table. Plunge the bit into each stile 1¾" from each end. The round corners left by the bit will be squared once the door frame is assembled.

13 Use a drill press to remove most of the waste for the mortises in each stile. Clean out the remainder with a sharp chisel. The mortise is ⅜"-wide by 1⅛"-deep and 1"-long. Refer to the illustration for the correct locations of these mortises.

14 The upper and lower rails require a ½"-wide by ½"-deep rabbet on one long edge. The middle rail requires the same rabbet cut on both long edges, as shown.

16 Round over the square corners on each rail tenon so they'll fit properly in the mortises. Use a wood file to take off a little at a time, then test fit the joint. Once all the tenons are correct, assemble the door frame with glue and clamps.

15 Form the tenons on both ends of each rail, paying attention to their positions on the end and middle rails. The tenons are cut ⅜"-thick to fit tightly in the stile mortises. Use a table saw and miter fence to nibble away the waste and form the tenons. Or, if you have a tenoning jig, make the cheek cut and complete the tenons with the jig.

17 Once the glue has set and the joints are secure, square the corners of each rabbet on the door frame. Use a sharp chisel on all eight corners.

18 Now is the best time to completely sand the door frame. Use a ⅜"-radius roundover bit to ease the front outside edges of the door.

19 | Verify your measurements before ordering the glass door panels and shelves. Rough cut the ⅜"-square wood moulding strips Q and R to length. They will be cut to the proper size and used to retain the glass door panels.

20 | Drill three 35mm-diameter holes in the door for the hinges. The holes are ⅛" from the door edge and deep enough to properly seat the hinges. I used a hidden hinge with a plate designed for face frame mounting. The hinges have a ½" overlay mounting plate. Apply the final finish now, as the best possible time is before the hardware and glass is installed. I used three coats of semigloss polyurethane to finish my case.

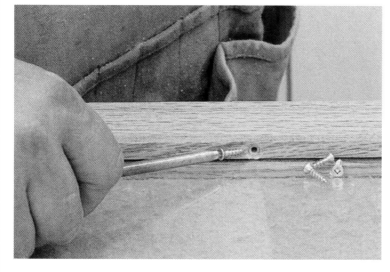

21 | Set the glass panels P in place on the door. Use the ⅜" wood strips to retain the glass and secure the strips with ⅝"-long screws. Drill holes in the wood strips for each screw, so they will be drawn tight to the door frame.

22 | Install the hinges on the door. Mount the door to the cabinet by holding it in its open position with a ⅛"-thick strip of wood between the door and face frame. Secure the mounting plate.

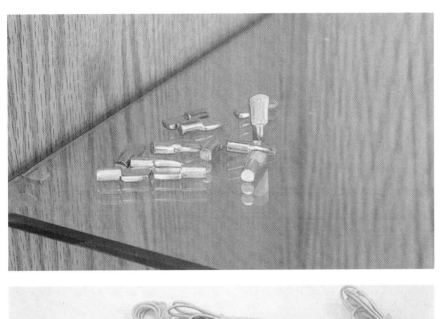

23 Brass pins that require a $\frac{3}{16}$"-diameter hole support the tempered glass shelves N. The edges on these shelves must be polished for safety reasons.

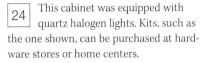

24 This cabinet was equipped with quartz halogen lights. Kits, such as the one shown, can be purchased at hardware stores or home centers.

Construction Notes

The cost of this project will be dramatically reduced if you don't require a door. But if you want a secure environment for your collection, and a bit more protection against dust, a door is the solution.

I didn't want attention drawn to the door, so I didn't install a handle. If you will be opening the door frequently, you may want to install one.

Installing a barrel lock on the door can further protect your collectibles. It won't stop a determined thief, but it will prevent excessive handling of your valuable collection.

These inexpensive locks are available at hardware stores and home centers. The cabinet is surprisingly stable and will stand unsupported. However, if there are small children in the home you might consider securing the case to the wall with a 3" screw through the back board into the wall stud.

I usually use red oak and apply three coats of polyurethane to most of my projects. The oak machines easily and is plentiful in my region, but any wood will work with this project. Choose a species that matches the other furniture in the room.

Biscuit joinery is an important part of this project, but as I previously stated, face nailing and glue or dowels are perfectly acceptable. Remember, there are dozens of ways to join wood, so find a method that suits your budget and experience.

The amount of material removed to form the rabbets is substantial. Where possible, make a series of small cuts instead of one large cut. It's a great deal safer and the results are often much better.

The door frame is made with mortises and tenons, and the glass is secured with wood strips. Once again, there are a number of door construction options that I will detail in this book, and any of them can be used with this project.

wall-mounted cabinet

Wall shelves often look like simple boxes that have been thrown together. The challenge is to design a functional shelf and keep it simple, while adding a little visual interest as well. I think that I have accomplished that goal by using a half-lap joint at the corners.

The shelves are adjustable and made of tempered glass to let light into every corner. The glass appears almost invisible so only the collection pieces are seen. That's an important point when displaying small items; some wall shelves overpower the collection.

This display shelf was built without doors, but you can install them if there is a requirement. I will discuss a few door options in the construction steps.

Keep this shelf in mind as a teaching project for a young woodworker. Not only can it be built with hand tools, it also illustrates the mechanical strength and usefulness of a half-lap joint. The edges can be formed with hand sanding, and the rabbets can be cut with a plane. Youngsters will love building this project and can always use a wall shelf in their room. Wall shelves, such as this one, are in demand. Be prepared to build a few more when you show this project to family and friends.

The salt and pepper shaker collection shown here is owned by Elsa Cawthray of Ottawa, Ontario.

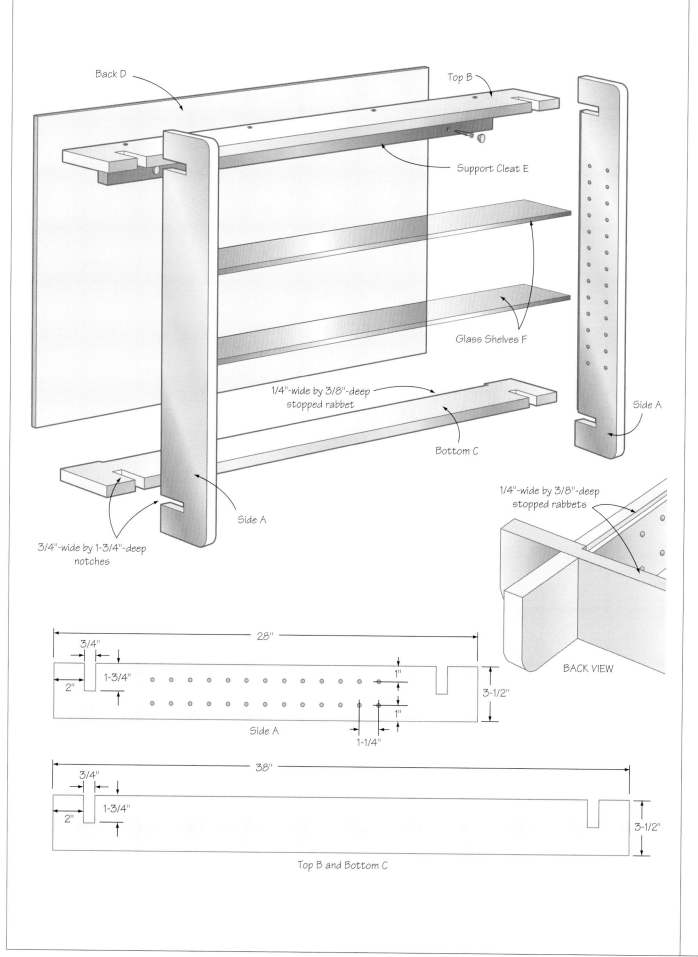

Back D

Top B

Support Cleat E

Glass Shelves F

Side A

1/4"-wide by 3/8"-deep
stopped rabbet

Bottom C

Side A

3/4"-wide by 1-3/4"-deep
notches

1/4"-wide by 3/8"-deep
stopped rabbets

BACK VIEW

28"

3/4"

1-3/4"

2"

1"

1"

3-1/2"

1-1/4"

Side A

38"

3/4"

1-3/4"

2"

3-1/2"

Top B and Bottom C

12 shelf pins for glass shelves

REFERENCE	QUANTITY	PART	STOCK	THICKNESS	(mm)	WIDTH	(mm)	LENGTH	(mm)
A	2	sides	oak	$\frac{3}{4}$	(19)	$3\frac{1}{2}$	(89)	28	(711)
B	1	tops	oak	$\frac{3}{4}$	(19)	$3\frac{1}{2}$	(89)	38	(965)
C	1	bottom	oak	$\frac{3}{4}$	(19)	$3\frac{1}{2}$	(89)	38	(965)
D	1	back	oak	$\frac{1}{4}$	(6)	$23\frac{1}{4}$	(591)	$33\frac{1}{4}$	(845)
E	1	support cleat	oak	$\frac{1}{2}$	(13)	1	(25)	$32\frac{1}{2}$	(826)
F	3	shelves	glass	$\frac{1}{4}$	(6)	$3\frac{1}{4}$	(83)	$32\frac{7}{16}$	(824)

1 Use No. 0 biscuits and glue to join the four mitered corners on the upper and lower case. Cut the biscuit slots, being careful not to puncture the outside face of the panel. Clamp each carcass until the adhesive sets.

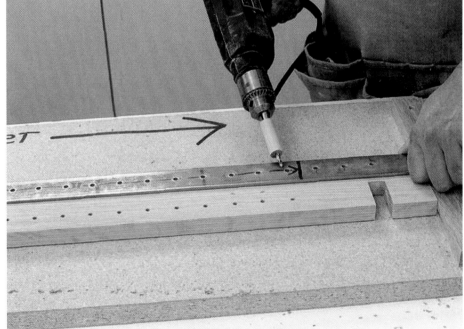

2 Drill two columns of holes in each side board for the adjustable shelf pins. The holes are 1" in from the front and back edges and $1\frac{1}{4}$" apart. Be sure the boards are oriented properly so the sides are mirror images. Measure and mark the hole positions, or build a simple jig that can be used for many other projects.

3 Use an object about 1½" in diameter and mark an arc on each corner of the top, bottom and side boards.

4 Use a belt sander to contour the corners by following the marks. Clamp the four boards together and form the corners. This technique ensures that all corners will be identical. Use this "ganged" sanding method when forming the contours on any project where there are a number of identical parts.

5 Dry fit the parts and mark a line showing the start and finish points that will be used when cutting rabbets on all pieces. The side, top and bottom boards all require a ¼"-wide by ⅜"-deep rabbet, which extends past the marks by ⅜". Cut the rabbets using a router table and straight bit.

6 Dry fit the parts again and square the corners with a sharp chisel.

7 Take the shelf frame apart for the last time and finish sand all parts. Apply glue to the notches and clamp the four pieces securely.

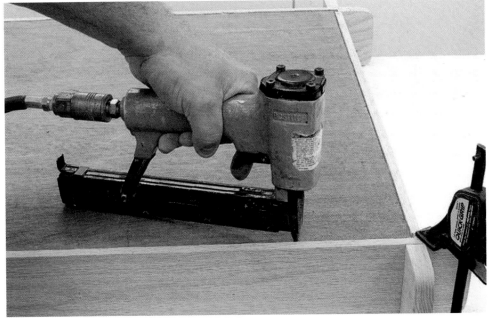

8 The back board D is installed in the rabbets and secured with glue and brad nails. If this board was properly cut with square corners it will align with the shelf frame.

9 The support cleat E is attached to the back underside of the top board. Use glue and two 1"-long screws in counterbored holes to secure the cleat. Fill the holes with wood plugs.

Construction Notes

This shelf unit can be secured to a wall with two 3" screws drilled through the support cleat and into a stud. Drill counterbored holes and use a wood button to cover the screw heads.

Apply a finish to your shelf unit and order the tempered glass shelves. I will be using three shelves that are $\frac{1}{4}$"-thick by 3"-deep and $32\frac{1}{16}$"-wide. However, your display may require a different number of shelves. Ask the glass supplier to polish the edges.

If you need a degree of security for your small collectibles, glass doors can be installed. There are a number of door options, the simplest being glass sliders in a track.

Plastic tracks are available at most hardware stores. The upper track is normally higher so the sliding doors can be lifted in and set in the bottom track. These tracks can be surface mounted or installed in routed grooves. Purchase the tracks before ordering the glass to verify the correct thickness.

Swinging glass doors may also be installed. Use hardware that includes hinges and handles, and doesn't re-

quire any holes drilled in the glass. It's great hardware and I've used it on many projects.

If you plan on using a wood frame door you can use the shorter version of hidden hinge hardware. The compact series hinges are the perfect hardware solution for wood frame and glass panel doors.

This shelf design can be easily altered to meet any requirements. Build the shelf taller or wider to suit your collectibles. The depth isn't limited to 1×4 stock, so use a wider board if needed. The shelf will be perfect as long as the notch depth is half the board width.

There are many ways to secure the shelf to a wall. If you don't like the cleat method, use a $\frac{1}{2}$"-thick back. Mounting screws can then be driven at any place on this thicker board. Or simple eyelets can be screwed into the top board and the unit suspended with screws. You may want to inset the back board and install wire hangers to secure the shelf. There are dozens of creative hanging methods, so select one that suits your needs.

Wood screw-hole buttons.

Sliding glass door tracks.

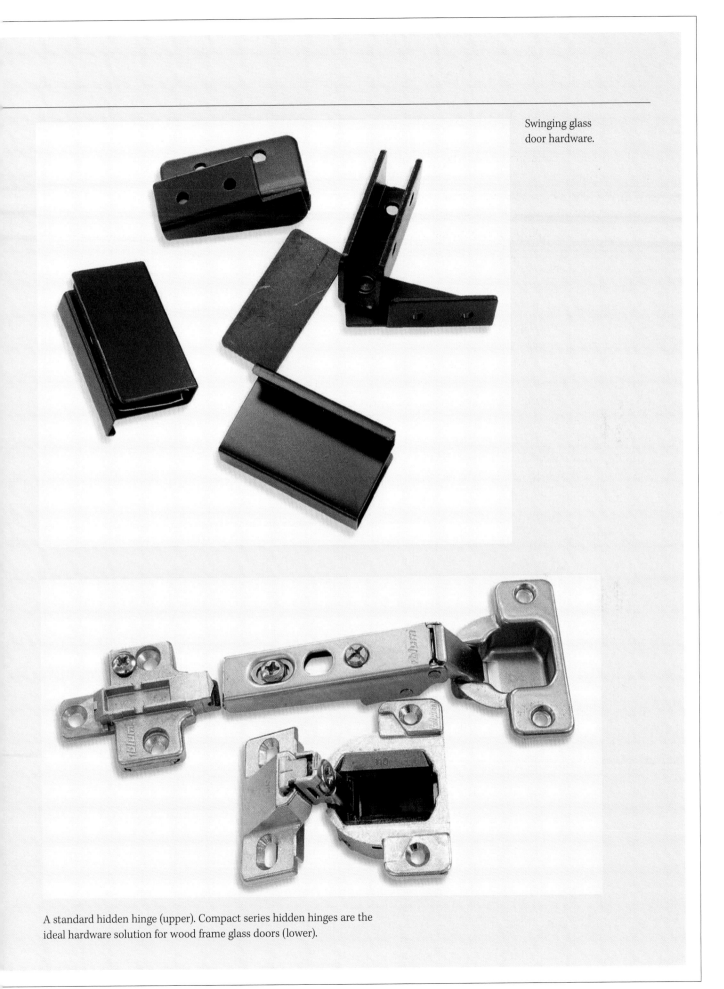

Swinging glass door hardware.

A standard hidden hinge (upper). Compact series hidden hinges are the ideal hardware solution for wood frame glass doors (lower).